Jacket Art:

USA 91 (detail) by Morris Shulman,
assemblage encaustic on panel,
25¼″ x 20″. Ceramic fragments were
cemented to a Masonite panel with
epoxy resin. Over the surface of the
fragments and the panel, encaustic
(an ancient formula of pigment and
beeswax) was flowed with the aid of
a torch.

MODERN MOSAIC TECHNIQUES

BY JANICE LOVOOS AND FELICE PARAMORE

Watson-Guptill Publications, New York

To Janice, with love, Felice
To Felice, with love, Janice

First published 1967 in New York by Watson-Guptill Publications,
a division of Billboard Publications, Inc.,
165 West 46 Street, New York, N.Y.

Manufactured in Japan
ISBN 0-8230-3120-9
Library of Congress Catalog Card Number: 67-13744
First Printing, 1967
Second Printing, 1969
Third Printing, 1972

ACKNOWLEDGMENTS

We are deeply indebted to the many artists and craftsmen who generously donated their time and effort, as well as photographs; to the students at Otis Art Institute who gave of their time and talents; to artist-instructors Richard Haines and Arthur Ames for assistance in setting up work projects; and especially to the artists who created original pieces for use in this book, namely F. Carlton Ball, Victor Casados, Janice Greenburg, Bonnie Jean Malcolm, Robert Ortlieb, and Robert Seyle.

We are also grateful to Helen Luitjens, head of the art department at Paul Revere Junior High School in Brentwood, California; to Gerald Citrin, art instructor at Le Conte Junior High School and to Dorothy McKee, fifth and sixth grade teacher at the Third Street School in Los Angeles, under whose guidance their students produced handsome work for inclusion in this book; and to Van Penney for gathering additional information on materials pertaining to the making of mosaics.

All have helped immeasurably toward cheering us on and bringing the book to a state of completion.

The Authors

PHOTO CREDITS

CONTENTS

PREFACE 11

INTRODUCTION 13

1. WHERE TO BEGIN

Work Area 17

Tesserae 18

Cutting Tools And Implements 19

Setting, Adhering, And Finishing
Materials 20

Grouting And Finishing 21

Supports 22

Other Materials And Equipment................ 22

Some Suggestions For Beginners 24

The Scope Of This Book 25

2. INDIRECT METHOD

Traditional Mural Technique 29

Color Sketch And Line Cartoon 30

Pasting The Tesserae 30

Installation 31

Demonstration Of Direct Techniques 32

Preliminary Drawings 32

Applying Tesserae 32

Preparing Panel 33

Transferring Tesserae To Panel 33

Grouting And Cleaning........................... 34

3. DIRECT METHOD

Requirements Of Project 45

Preliminary Sketch 46
Executing The Design............................. 46
Color And Texture 46

4. **SANDCASTING**

Placing Tesserae In Box 57
Pouring Magnesite Over Tesserae 58
Separating Panel From Box...................... 58

5. **FOUND OBJECTS**

Experimenting With The Design
    Elements.. 77
Found Objects From Nature 78
Examples In This Chapter 78

6. **CERAMIC MOSAIC**

Forming The Ceramic Pieces 97
Adhering The Ceramic Pieces 98
Ceramic Mosaic Relief 100
Making The Leaf Forms 102
Completing The Design 102
Ceramic Mosaic Wall Panel 104
Cutting And Firing 104
Assembling And Mounting 104

7. **WOOD MOSAICS**

Wood Mosaic Reliefs 108
Wood Carving And Wood Mosaics 110
Planning The Design................................110

Carving The Wood Pieces..........................110
Completing The Panel 110
Wood Constructions 114

8. **NAIL MOSAICS**

Types Of Nails 118
Textures 118

9. **MOSAIC SCULPTURE**

Modeling The Basic Form..........................125
Setting The Tesserae 126
Inlay 129
Modeling Wax Form 129
Completing The Inlay 130
Scale Models For Presentation 130

10. **MOSAIC TECHNIQUES FOR SCHOOLS**

Mosaics From The Kitchen........................136
Eggshell Mosaics 136
Some Suggestions About Color.................136
Paper Mosaics 137
Planning The Design................................137
Rubber Cement 137
Paper Mosaics By Children 137

BIBLIOGRAPHY   163

LIST OF SUPPLIERS   165

INDEX   167

PREFACE

In an exciting, fast changing world of new values and concepts, the arts invariably reflect the imaginative and experimental qualities of our time.

The strong and expressive feeling in today's abstract concepts—inherent in all of the contemporary arts—permeates every medium in the graphic arts.

Janice Lovoos and Felice Paramore, in their enthusiastic approach to the arts, have cut a fine cross-section through the special field of mosaic in their new book *Modern Mosaic Techniques*.

They have clearly shown, through the selection of materials for this book, that mosaic concepts have broadened dramatically in the twentieth century; there is now no limitation in the materials that the artist may choose for use in his work. The book should assist both professional and avocational artists in discovering broad new means for expression. Decoration to please the eye—or a serious effort to express great ideas—can be enhanced by a new attitude toward the materials used.

To the working designer, new combinations of materials offer more expressive means for solving today's problems, far beyond the ancient techniques utilizing only glass and stone.

This is not a pedantic book dealing merely with the techniques of mosaic, but is primarily concerned with awakening the thought and spirit of artists, both young and old, toward the discovery of more rewarding means of expression.

Millard Sheets

11

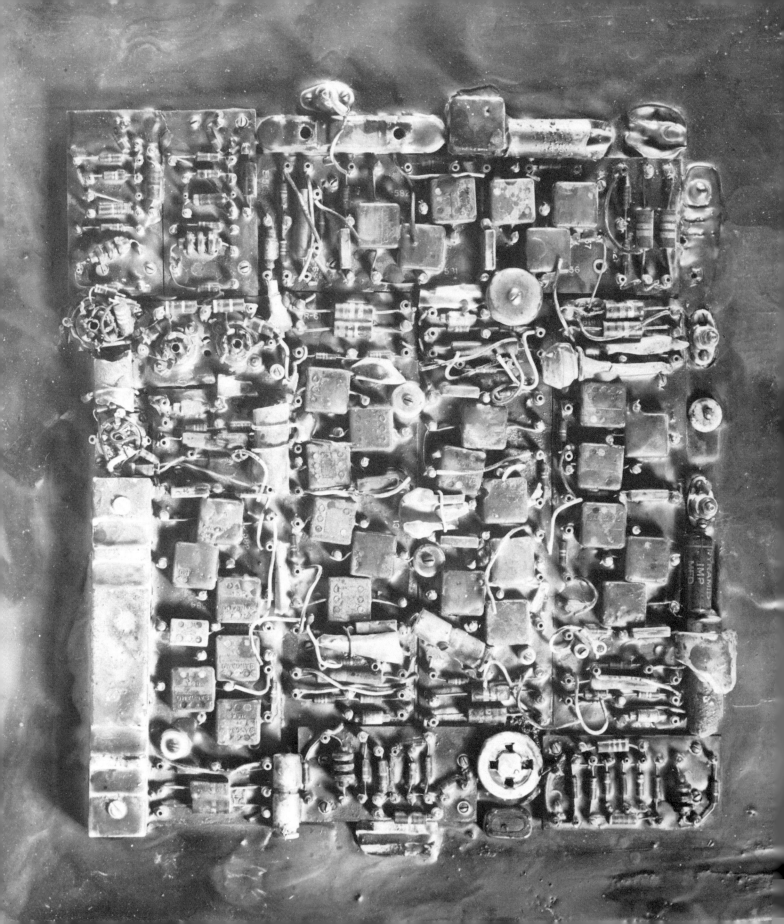

ASSEMBLAGE by Morris Shulman. The artist has cemented scrap electronic parts to a Masonite panel — the adhesive is epoxy resin — and coated parts and background with richly colored encaustic. For another example of this technique, see the color frontispiece.

The making of mosaics has been the concern of craftsmen for at least 5000 years and there is little denying the fascination this ancient art holds for artist and laymen alike. Whether it is the red or black and white pavements of Lisbon, the fantastic Tower of Watts, or a table top inlaid with glass tesserae, mosaics appeal to our imagination.

ROMAN AND BYZANTINE MOSAICS

One may think first of mosaic as church decoration. As religious art, mosaic reached its peak of development during the Byzantine period, with its lace-like carvings and jewel-like mosaic work, an era when Byzantine craftsmen introduced an elegance and intricacy of pattern hitherto unknown.

In its earliest beginnings, however, mosaic leaned strongly in the direction of simplicity and quiet coloration. In the 1st century after Christ, limestone and marble were used almost to the exclusion of other materials. Floor mosaics carried scrolls, border and geometric patterns, often simply in black and white. Excellent examples of floor mosaics, some of them produced as early as the 2nd century B.C., remain in the ancient city of Pompeii.

But in the more opulent Byzantine era, monotones gave way to brilliant color. White and soft hued backgrounds were replaced by shimmering gold. The accelerated glass industry manufactured tesserae in literally hundreds of shades.

DECLINE OF MOSAICS IN THE RENAISSANCE

With the coming of the Renaissance and its resuscitation of painting and other art forms, mosaic became almost obscured. If decorators of that period employed mosaic at all, it was in an attempt to emulate painting; bits of glass and marble were set so closely together that the original purpose of the material was disregarded.

Among the mosaic murals emerging from that period of ostentatious design were two of the large murals in St. Mark's, Venice, whose designs were said to have been made by Titian. Yet, despite the skillful execution of designs by one of the greatest painters of the Venetian school, this mosaic mural — and comparable wall decorations of that era — made mosaic something it was never intended to be: a medium with which to create pictorial effects — an imitation of painting. Although imitation may be a sincere form of flattery, these "mosaic paintings" also became a reason for hastening mosaic into near oblivion.

With little or no use for the multi-colored tesserae they had developed, glass factories now discontinued their manufacture as the art of mosaic declined. Only the work of past generations — fortunately, there was an abundance — remained as proof that mosaic had once been a vital art. Only in the manufacture of inexpensive jewelry did the craft persist; this production has continued to the present day.

REVITAL OF MOSAICS
IN 19th AND 20th CENTURIES

It was not until the middle of the 19th century that mosaic began to reassume a role of importance. In the field of mural decoration — most of it Venetian or Venetian-influenced — much of the actual work was executed by Italian artists imported for that purpose.

Typical examples of murals produced during that era are to be found in England: in the reredos (altar screen) of Westminster Abbey, for example. In the main hall of Parliament are others made from designs by Sir Alfred Poynter, an English painter who also worked in stained glass, mosaic, and ceramics. More successful were the mosaics designed for the American Church of Rome, by Sir Edward Burne Jones, an English painter and designer whose influence was strongly felt during his productive life span and for several decades following. Yet even in the work of so skilled a designer, joints between the closely set tesserae were almost invisible, thereby creating a polished surface that neglected the material; the murals were more nearly illustrations than the pure design for which mosaic is best suited.

With the quickening pace of American industry, commercial tile began making its appearance. Factories in Pennsylvania, Ohio, New Jersey, and California accelerated their production to meet growing demands for a material that enjoyed almost immediate success and which, in turn, gave impetus to an increased interest in mosaics.

But this flurry of activity was quickly subdued by the coming of World War II and its accompanying curtailment of critical materials. It was not until 1950, when materials were once again made available, that serious interest in mosaic was reborn.

TRADITIONAL AND MODERN TECHNIQUES

In making mosaics today, two traditional methods are still employed: the *direct* and the *indirect* techniques.

The *direct* method implies that the tesserae are set *directly* into the cement, sand, glue, or whatever material is used. A rough sketch may be followed. A more experienced craftsman may work spontaneously from an idea in mind.

The *indirect* or *reverse* method is so-called because the design is first drawn or painted on paper onto which the tesserae are tentatively glued; the whole thing is then turned upside-down into the wet binding material, thus causing the design to be *in reverse* from the original drawing. This method is essentially the same as that used more than 500 years ago.

But today, mosaic, like other art forms, has broken with tradition and 20th century artists are constantly seeking new directions in pursuing the ancient crafts. Their work may verge on collage, assemblage, and constructions. Or they may combine mosaic with ceramics, fabric, and painted designs to achieve different effects.

To obtain materials, cracked china or broken tiles are pounded into smaller pieces. Fragments of wood are drafted into service. The eager mosaicist combs the beaches and city streets on "trash day," hopeful of finding suitable materials. The kitchen yields dried foods. Scraps of colored paper are considered suitable. Modern chemistry has also helped to accelerate this uninhibited creative outburst by producing new mortars, glues, and other materials that work easily and effectively.

Because of this emancipation of the modern craftsman, the word *mosaic* itself must now be reconsidered in its broadest meaning. Mosaic is no longer confined to a prescribed way of working with specific materials, but expanded to include *almost anything*. The modern mosaicist can be as original and uninhibited as he dares!

Only the future can properly evaluate what he will have accomplished. It remains with the artist — his individuality and the degree of his artistic integrity showing through his technical skills — to produce work that the future will pronounce significant, or mere technical display.

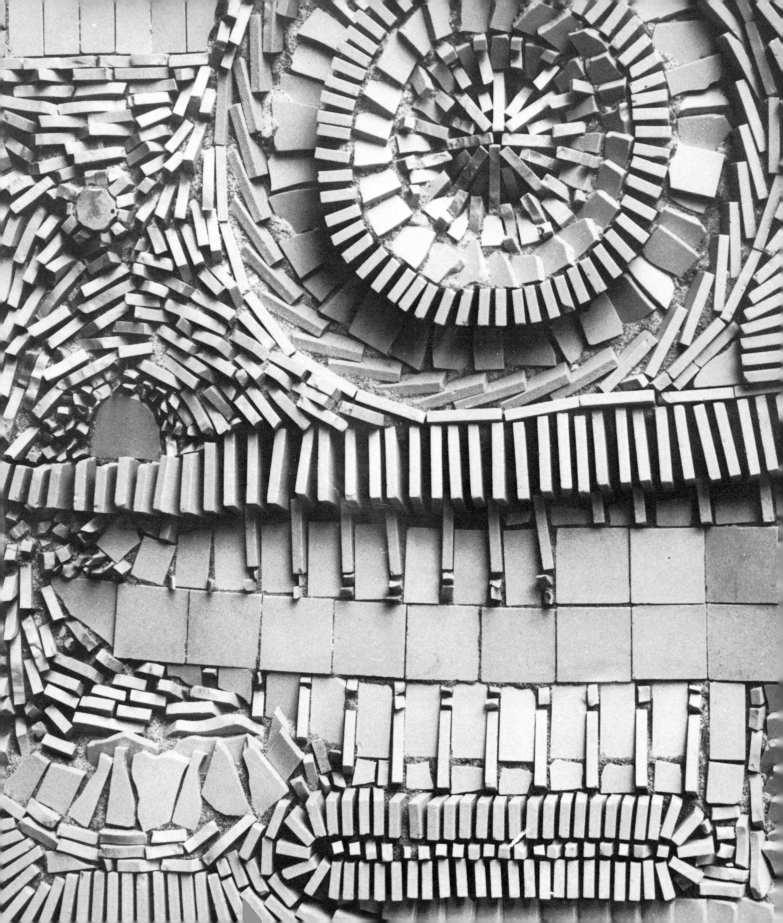

1. WHERE TO BEGIN

There is an eternal fascination about mosaic that appeals to artist and layman, young and old alike. Perhaps part of our pleasure in admiring and creating decorative surfaces (such as mosaic) is an outgrowth of our experience as children — putting picture puzzles together, building castles out of blocks. In each instance, many separate pieces have been combined or placed together in some manner to produce a unified whole, a *mosaic* of differing colors, varied textures and shapes. This immediately arrests our eye and stimulates our imagination. Whatever the fascination, it has been sufficient to bring about a lively 20th century renaissance of the ancient craft and to introduce many modern mosaic techniques, as well as variations and offshoots of old methods.

WORK AREA

To begin your mosaic project, you won't need a professional workshop or studio to produce good work. Handsome pieces have emerged from the most unimpressive surroundings. But you *will* need a sturdy table or work bench that feels comfortable to you. You will also need adequate storage space for your materials and tools.

Pick an area that has plenty of light. A section of a garage, an outdoor patio, an infrequently used room inside the house, even one end of a kitchen —

MOSAIC PANEL by Robert Seyle, sandcasting. Here texture and contrast were achieved by imaginative use of ordinary bathroom tile, all in closely related shades of gray. There is a wonderful feeling of movement throughout the design in which tiles were set at varying heights and in all directions. Square, oblong, and free form shapes were used, many set on end.

all have been successfully adapted to working and storage areas.

If you are working with gritty materials such as sand or cement, it is advisable to spread several thicknesses of newspaper or a painter's drop cloth on the floor. Or if you prefer, protect it with a covering of cardboard: Try to keep the working area as clean as possible.

Keep your tiles or other setting materials separated in glass containers so you can locate, at a glance, whatever you are looking for.

Because modern mosaicists use such an infinite variety of materials — far beyond the traditional tiles and adhesives — no list of materials and equipment could possibly be complete. However, here are some notes about materials and tools which mosaicists commonly use and which you may want to try, depending upon *what* you plan to make and *how* you plan to make it.

TESSERAE

Tesserae are the tiles, or cubes, used in making traditional mosaics. The name is derived from the Greek word, tesserae, meaning four. The singular form is tessera.

Byzantine enamel tesserae, known as smalti, are handmade and imported from Europe. This is the preferred material of professional mosaicists, coming in literally hundreds of shades, rectangular in shape, and irregular in size (approximately ½" x ⅜" x 5⁄16"). The price varies with the color, quality, and amount purchased, but this is one of the more expensive mosaic materials. Smalti tesserae are ready to use just as you buy them in bulk. Purchased from distributors in the United States, they are sold by the pound; imported from Italy, they are sold by the kilo. They may be halved, quartered, or cut into triangular (or even circular) shapes with the proper tools.

Venetian glass tile is pressed or cast glass, first produced in Venice. It is available in uniform size tiles, ¾" x ¾". It comes pasted onto sheets of paper approximately one foot square. It is also sold in bulk by the pound. Although it comes in a wide range of colors, it is not as handsome, but far less expensive than the more elegant, Byzantine tesserae.

Marble tesserae (marme) are another equally handsome, but expensive import from Italy.

Ceramic tiles are the least expensive of all mosaic tesserae. They are ideal for the beginner. They come in ¾" squares; their surface may be glossy or matte. Look for them in stores where tile setting is done. There you may also find scrap material sold by the pound. Ceramic tiles should be soaked in water for a few minutes and carefully dried before using; otherwise they will absorb moisture from the embedding material and come loose.

Glass: don't overlook the possibilities of using window glass in your mosaics. Shards of stained glass (sometimes sold as scrap material where stained glass windows are made), old colored glass bottles (cut or broken with a hammer inside a heavy burlap sack), and odd bits and fragments also work well.

To cut flat sheets of glass, use the kind of glass cutter that has a wheel on one end of the handle and a round iron ball on the other. Lay the glass flat on a solid table or bench. Score the glass, making lines about ½" apart. Draw the cutter over your scored lines, being careful to press evenly and not bear down too hard — just enough to "bite" the glass. Then score the glass *across* the vertical lines already scored. Thump it with the metal ball and the pieces will fall out.

Spraying or brushing paint on window glass, or on any clear sheet glass, is another way of obtaining the colors you want. You can achieve an unusually handsome effect by combining pieces of glass with squares of ceramic tile.

It doesn't matter if the sheet glass or clear plastic has flaws. You will probably conceal the flaws anyway, and the cost of flawed or imperfect glass is less than the cost of perfect pieces.

This material may usually be acquired very cheaply, but care and sensitive judgment must be exercised in its use, or it will lack luminosity and appear dull and cloudy. Its brilliance depends on the amount of light that is reflected back through it from the setting bed. It is most effective set into white cement. It should never be set into a black mastic; the darker the setting, the duller the tesserae will appear.

Be sure to keep your glass cutters sharp. Store them in turpentine. If you want to adhere glass to glass, or to clear plastic, use epoxy cement, a clear liquid plastic which, when mixed with an amber colored liquid catalyst, will form a hard, permanent bond. Acetone will clean up unnecessary spots left by the epoxy.

The materials mentioned above may be used in either the direct or indirect techniques (Chapters 2, 3, and 4). Other techniques utilize *found objects* (which includes almost anything found in pieces or fragmented form), pebbles, rocks, dried vegetables, paper, pasta — in short, any material that is practical and interesting for creating a mosaic or mosaic-like surface.

CUTTING TOOLS AND IMPLEMENTS

Hutch and scaling hammer: probably the oldest tools used in the art of mosaic are the hutch and scaling hammer. These are the cutting tools with which tesserae are traditionally cut. The hutch consists of a wide metal blade imbedded in a sturdy block, with the sharp edge of the blade extending about 3″ above the block. Italian craftsmen traditionally use a wide coal chisel imbedded in the end of a log cut to about knee height. The log stands with the sharp edge of the chisel protruding from the end and is just the right height for the seated mosaic worker to cut tesserae on.

The tessera is held between the thumb and forefinger and placed, widest side down, across the edge of the hutch blade at just the angle that is desired. Then, with a sharp, quick blow, the blade of the scaling hammer (sometimes called a chipping hammer) is brought down on the tessera in line with, and directly above, the hutch blade. With practice, the cuts will become very accurate.

Cut nippers have become very popular with many mosaic artists because they are easier to use. They are mechanically similar to a pair of pliers, but the working end consists of two vertically aligned blades that open and close.

You will find a selection of various cutters and nippers at supply stores that stock mosaic materials, and at large hardware stores. If you are willing to pay a little more for carbide tipped nippers, they will outlast others. Cutters with longer handles are easier to use.

The finest quality cut nippers are made by the L. S. Starrett Company, 48 Commerce Street, Springfield, N. J. Starrett cut nippers, series No. 235, are available in 5½″ and 7″ lengths.

The usual procedure for cutting is to place the tile (or tessera) between the thumb and forefinger at a 90° angle, allow the converging blades to bite just inside the edge of the tessera (turned to the desired angle of cut); then quick pressure is applied and the tessera will split at the desired angle. Cut it into two halves; then you can cut the halves in two to make quarters. You can also cut across the tile *diagonally* to make two triangles, then cut them in two to make triangular quarters.

Some tiles, as well as some colors, are easier to cut than others. It may take a little experimenting to produce accurate, clean cuts, but when done right, this does give your work a more professional appearance. Smalti are more difficult to cut with cut nippers than Venetian glass tile.

Smaller pieces are harder to cut and to handle.

But if they are used, try not to set them along the edges of a piece where they are likely to fall out and get lost. The beginner should try to keep his cuts simple.

SETTING, ADHERING, AND FINISHING MATERIALS

Having selected your tesserae or other material for executing your design, you must obviously have some form of adhesive that will hold the pieces to the surface of the panel, wall, or other support; and if the indirect method of setting the tesserae is to be used, you must have a temporary pasteup adhesive.

Glue: the glue that has been used for centuries as a temporary adhesive to paste the tesserae to the paper in the indirect method is a home-made brew. It consists of a 10% solution of gum arabic, plus blackstrap molasses, and flour. Gum arabic crystals may be purchased in art supply shops. The proper strength of gum arabic solution is made by dissolving one ounce (by weight) of gum arabic crystals in ten ounces (by volume) of boiling water. Stir frequently until the crystals are dissolved. Strain the resulting solution through four layers of cheesecloth.

Mix one part gum arabic solution with two parts wheat or rye flour, and add one part blackstrap molasses. The resulting solution should be thick and viscous, but of a consistency that can be applied with a paintbrush.

For small projects that will *not* have to be lifted from the work table to be set into the cement bed, a simpler glue solution is described in Chapter 2 by Victor Casados. This formula excludes the gum arabic solution.

Cement, mortar, stucco, or concrete: the permanent setting materials for mosaic are many and varied in their characteristics. Until modern times, mosaics were set almost exclusively in a cement and sand mixture, with lime sometimes added (to mixtures that were not exposed to the weather) to make the mixture easier to handle.

Mixtures of Portland cement and sand make excellent setting beds for mosaic, either set by the indirect method or by the direct method. For work that is not to be exposed to the weather, a mixture of one part Portland cement to three parts sand is correct. This mixture may be made easier to work with by including hydrated lime in the proportion of one part lime, two parts cement, six parts sand. For work that *is* to be exposed to the weather, waterproof Portland cement should be used in the proportions stated above, and no lime may be used.

When lime is added to the cement and sand mix, it is known as *mortar* or *stucco*. When pebbles and stones are added, it is known as *concrete*.

The proper quantity of water to use in the mix is determined by the aggregate that is used. If lime is used, then slightly less water should be used. The liquid mix should be thick enough to stand up as a lump on a trowel, but liquid enough to show a film of water on its surface.

Latex cement: a much stronger setting bed results from adding liquid latex to the dry aggregate mix instead of water. Mix to the same consistency as if water were used. This produces a very tough, flexible, adhesive layer for the tesserae to rest in. It is particularly advantageous where a *thin* setting bed is desired.

Magnesite is a hard cement which comes in powder form. When mixed with magnesium chloride, it is used as a bonding agent and/or grout. It is not practical for small panels. Magnesite is available at builders' supply stores.

Mastic, an organic adhesive manufactured specifically for the installation of tile, sets quickly, is water-repellent, but is highly flammable.

Epoxy resin, mentioned before as a good adhesive to bond glass to glass, has excellent bonding properties and has proven to be useful in bonding a very great variety of materials. It sets inert and is absolutely permanent even under extreme weather conditions.

Epoxy is a clear resin which, when mixed in the proper proportion with a catalyst, or hardener (an amber liquid), will harden to a tough, durable plastic with extraordinary adhesive properties. It may be purchased in small quantities in twin tubes at hardware stores and hobby shops. Large quantities may be purchased directly from the Shell Chemical Company, Dow Chemical Company, the Chemical Division of General Mills, and other chemical companies. The epoxy-catalyst combinations that are available through retail outlets all set very quickly, within about thirty minutes. A twelve hour catalyst, known as Versimid, is available from General Mills.

Epoxy resins should be used with caution. They must be used only in well ventilated areas and contact with the skin should be avoided. Prolonged work with epoxy resins should be avoided. The cleaning agent for epoxy and catalyst is Acetone, followed by soap and water.

Polyvinyl acetate adhesives (white glues) are sold under various trade names. They are water-resistant, and are available at hardware stores and hobby shops. Milky white plastic glues have excellent bonding properties on porous and slightly textured materials. They dry water-resistant, but not waterproof. These glues will *not* bond smooth glass permanently.

Casein glues are milky in color. Once applied, they become transparent when dry, but are less water-resistant than polyvinyl acetate substances.

GROUTING AND FINISHING

In any art medium, the individual stamp of the artist is always present in his work, even though basic rules or standard procedures are adhered to. So it is with mosaic. Mosaicists have their own feeling about materials, color, and ways of working, gained through the years of their individual experience.

To grout or not to grout, for instance, is a personal choice. Grout is the substance that is worked into the spaces between the tesserae as they are being set into the bonding agent, or after the setting is completed. This part of the setting of a mosaic is known as *grouting*; consequently, the substance used, whatever it may be, is called grout. Thus, a mosaic set into a cement sand bed is grouted with the same mixture that is used for the setting bed; the cement simply works its way up into the separations between the tesserae as the mosaic is tamped into the setting bed.

Mosaics that have been set into a bed of mastic or epoxy resin are better grouted with a material *different* from the setting bed. A mixture of lime, cement, and fine sand (as described for the setting bed) is standard practice.

A ready-mixed grout, which may be purchased in art and craft shops, is good for beginners. Ready-mixed grout is available in a wide range of colors.

Plaster and spackle are not permanent materials to grout mosaics with.

Some artists prefer not to grout at all, claiming that the gaps between the tesserae have an interest of their own, strengthening the design and adding texture. Excellent adhesives are manufactured today, some especially designed for specific materials, so that tesserae will hold fast to backgrounds of metal, wood, masonry, composition board, or plastic, making grouting unnecessary. If the piece is to be used outdoors, however, it must be grouted if it is expected to withstand the onslaughts of the elements. This is also true of trays, ashtrays — any object that receives hard usage.

You can make your own grouting material by combining one to three parts of hydrated lime to six parts of Portland cement (white or gray) and six to twelve parts of fine sand. When the dry ingredients are thoroughly mixed, add water gradually — just as you do with prepared cake mix — until it has reached a creamy consistency, not unlike thin cake batter. But buying prepared grout in a sack is the simplest method, especially for the beginner who has enough to think about just getting started.

Spread the grout into the crevices with a palette knife, with a brush, or even with your hands, making certain that the grout has completely filled all the cracks. Remove the excess grout with a dampened cloth, a sponge, or the kind of rubber spatula you use to scrape dishes. Keep gently clearing the surface and removing bits of surplus as you work.

Grout may be left white, or it may be colored with a dry mix that you can buy where you buy your grout. White grout gives a strong contrast and therefore has a tendency to detract from the design itself. Use a grout color closely related to a predominating color in your mosaic to help integrate the over-all pattern.

Never rush the drying process. Allow the grouted panel to dry for twenty-four hours if possible. After four hours, the mosaic should be wetted again so that moisture may be returned to the grout to keep it from setting up brittle.

To clean the mosaic, you should have on hand plenty of soft rags, steel wool, tweezers, and a brush. Clear water and soft rags are usually used to clean the tile. But never use detergent.

The professional way to clean a mosaic after grouting is with a full strength solution of muriatic acid, and this should be done about twelve to eighteen hours after the grouting has been completed. The acid may be applied liberally with old rags tied to sticks. Wear goggles, rubber gloves, and old clothes. Allow the acid to remain on the panel for about ten minutes. Then rinse the panel with a solution of two tablespoons of baking soda to eight ounces of water. Clean with clear water and dry. This cleaning method makes the tesserae sparkle and also brings out the true beauty of the tile.

Some artists prefer the more subtle, duller shades and obtain them by giving the finished mosaic an oil base stain made by combining oil paint (sienna, brown, gray or gray-green, all will do the trick) with turpentine. After allowing the stain to set for a few moments, the surplus may be wiped off with a soft rag.

SUPPORTS

Unless you are working directly on a wall, you must select an appropriate surface to which your tesserae or other mosaic elements will be cemented, glued, etc. Here are three reliable supports in widespread use:

Plywood: a hard-surfaced wood — such as plywood, made of several sheets of veneer glued together — is excellent for a backing or base, ½″ or ¾″ thickness for small panels, ¾″ to 1″ for large panels. You can obtain plywood at lumber yards, building supply stores, hobby or craft shops, in panels already cut to various standard sizes.

Marine plywood: the waterproof ingredients in Marine plywood make a better base than ordinary plywood if your mosaic piece is to be used outdoors or exposed to dampness.

Masonite: this composition board is suitable for backing small mosaics. In addition to the above sources, it may also be purchased at art supply stores.

OTHER MATERIALS AND EQUIPMENT

Here are a variety of other things you may find useful. Once again, you won't need them *all;* different ones are handy for different jobs.

Tweezers are wonderful for moving small pieces about, for holding tesserae while applying adhesives, and for pushing pieces into final positions on the panel. Long-pronged tweezers are excellent but smaller "eyebrow" types also work well.

Palette knife: this is the same flexible tool that artists use, made of thin metal with a wooden handle — fine for spreading grout, for working it in between the tesserae, and for other odd jobs.

Putty knife: this is for working with grout, patching, etc. Find it at hardware stores, art supply stores, or hobby shops.

Trowel: you can use the small tool for spreading grout and embedding materials. This is available in hardware stores under the name of "mason's trowel" (pointed) or "plasterer's trowel" (square end).

Screw driver: this is useful for remedying mistakes after the mastic is set; for removing tesserae badly set, etc.

Spatula: small ones are used for buttering tesserae with adhesive. Larger rubber spatulas (dish scrapers) are used for working grout into the crevices and spaces between tesserae.

Scoop chisel: use a ½" round scoop chisel for scooping out wood and for very deep relief cutting on wood.

Riffler: this is a tool designed to go around corners and other difficult areas on wood — a curved file for very shallow carving or in-carving.

Electric drill: use this for finishing and refining wood.

Electric sander: this is a time saver for refining and sanding electrically.

The last four implements are used on wood. Electric sanders and drills are not necessarily a part of mosaic making, but are used on special jobs involving wood. As you discover which tools you like most to work with and as you evolve your own style, you may even start inventing tools and equipment of your own.

Tracing paper is a transparent paper that enables you to see at once how your design will look in *reverse.* Tracing paper comes in several weights and in a number of different sized pads, as well as in rolls. Buy it at art supply stores, architects' supply stores, and at some stationery shops.

Cardboard: the thin variety (such as laundries use for backing men's shirts) is ideal for cutting out forms to be used in working out your design.

Turpentine (oil of turpentine or spirits of turpentine) is a fluid used for painting with oil paint, available at art supply stores, paint or hardware stores.

Eye goggles give inexpensive protection for your eyes while cutting or pounding tesserae which may chip and fly about.

Hydrochloric (muriatic) acid is a strong, inorganic acid sometimes used to clean mosaic. It is also used to clean metal, but changes its color somewhat.

Baking soda, mixed with water, is used to neutralize the acid. A liquid soda solution should always be at hand when acid is being used.

Hard paste wax, the same kind used for polishing furniture, gives a soft sheen to ceramic mosaic.

Library paste may be used for temporary setting of tiles, used in the direct method.

Sandpaper: regular commercial paper is used for finishing and polishing.

Brushes of various kinds (from discarded paint brushes to scrub brushes, bottle brushes, and the like) are useful for many odd jobs of spreading, embedding, cleaning, etc.

Sealer is a protective preparation to finish mosaic and to seal plywood to avoid warping. This silicone preparation is sold at hardware stores, building supply stores, and hobby shops.

Varnish and shellac: these are a protective finish for mosaics, but not good for table tops, trays, etc., which may come into contact with liquids that might be spilled; shellac then acquires a white haze. Varnish is superior to shellac.

Builder's cloth (or *hardware cloth*) is a heavy screen mesh used for reinforcement purposes in making mosaics.

Marble dust: tesserae, marble chips, bits of glass, etc., ground to powder form, are sometimes used as grout to fill spaces between the tesserae and the base in the *direct* technique.

Styrofoam is an extruded plastic foam that may be carved, used in making forms and molds, and cut into definite shapes to be included in a design. It comes in boards and billets at building supply stores and plastic supply houses, and in various shapes at hobby shops.

Hydrocal is a material something like plaster of Paris, but more durable for carving, creating forms, making molds, etc. Buy it at paint stores, and some art supply stores.

Oil base stain can just be oil paint mixed with turpentine to a thin solution, used to wash over or stain a surface, usually to soften the color or dull a too-shiny surface.

Bowls, in an assortment of sizes, are useful for mixing grout and other materials, for storing, and for any number of purposes. Those made of plastic are most satisfactory.

Sponges, purchased almost anywhere, are useful for an infinite number of odd jobs, including wiping away excess grout.

Steel wool and rags: these useful household objects are helpful in cleaning mosaics and the working area.

Nails are needed for nailing strips of wood molding around the edges of mosaic panels to achieve a professional finish. In this book, many types of nails are also used as an art medium.

Garnet paper is more durable than regular sandpaper for finishing wood (purchased at hardware or building supply stores).

Metallic oxides are permanent coloring pigments, dry-mixed with grout, which is white, to obtain various shades and tints. Available at chemical supply stores.

Reducing glass: a concave glass (the opposite of a magnifying glass), a reducing glass shows a mosaic panel (or design) reduced in size, so that the artist may see the over-all effect of a panel, rather than just the details.

Sheet metal: thin sheets of various metals — such as brass, copper, aluminum, or tin — may be cut to desired shapes with tin snips for use in metal mosaics, mixed media mosaics, or assemblages.

SOME SUGGESTIONS FOR BEGINNERS

If you've had any training in art or design, that's a head start! But people with no training at all have turned out creditable mosaic designs. So, if you have no art training, don't let that stop you.

If you live in an area where you can see mosaics in shops, stores, or galleries, observe the talents and workmanship of the artists you most admire. To help you learn something about design, there are endless books on the subject in your public library. There are handsome printed volumes showing the ancient mosaics; although they are often beyond the technical means of the beginner, they will still give him something if he studies them carefully — if nothing more than to gain an idea of what the finest work in this field can be.

Observe nature; take note of the beauty and simplicity of its design. Even a single leaf pattern can be a handsome idea for a mosaic.

If you have never worked with mosaic before, it is best to start by covering a small area or decorating a small object. You might begin by setting tesserae on an unglazed ashtray or tea tile. Or you may wish to refurbish a discarded soap dish, or even a door knob, by giving it a new surface. In short, anything that will be benefited by the addition of mosaic — but keep early projects small and simple!

Later on, when you try more ambitious jobs that require large panels, use ¾" or 1" plywood. Protect it from warping with a prime coat of sealer. You can spread the surface with a coat of mastic and press each tile down firmly into the wet background material. Or you can cover the back of each tile with glue (this is called *buttering*, and a palette knife is ideal for this purpose) and set it in place. A flat, smooth surface is necessary only on pieces such as serving trays or table tops. On other pieces, an uneven surface is often desirable because it accentuates the handmade qualities. The somewhat primitive appearance adds to its charm.

With more experience, you may wish to make a table top or a new splash board surface for your bathroom. In making a design for a table top, draw directly on the wood surface, keeping pencil lines from smudging with a coat of shellac. If the table is to be used for serving, it is best to use marine plywood to protect the board from warping if drinks or other liquids are to be served on it. You may, if you wish, reinforce the surface beneath the tiles by using builder's cloth (hardware cloth). If metal edging is to be used, or legs added, protect them from stain, mortar, etc., by wrapping them with masking tape.

One can easily become carried away with detail in working on mosaics, for each segment is fascinating to watch as it develops. In order to produce a well integrated over-all design, one must occasionally stand back and view it from a distance. This can be done only after a section is finished and *dry*. Then, standing it upright, you see how the piece will look hanging on a wall.

Looking through a reducing glass — which reduces your design by making it look farther away, thus minimizing the detail — is also helpful. The design should carry from across the room.

Starting with a simple project will familiarize you with the materials. Because you are certain to enjoy handling some materials more than others, working on small pieces is economical. When you have experimented on several pieces, this is the time to order larger amounts of materials.

A beginner will be able to produce interesting pieces in a relatively short time. The hours spent in learning to handle mosaic properly are few, compared to the time spent learning other crafts. Almost immediately, you can see the results of your labor. But the beginner should not attempt a design that is too complicated, one whose concept and technique require skill far in advance of his knowledge. If he does, he may become discouraged before he has really started.

If there is an opportunity to have even a little professional instruction, it will be encouraging to the beginner. There are professional workshops that charge a modest fee to learn the basics of mosaic making. There are night classes in public schools, as well as daytime sessions and adult education classes for those who seek expert guidance.

THE SCOPE OF THIS BOOK

The two basic methods of making mosaics are both set forth in the following chapters, with text and pictures showing how to proceed with either the

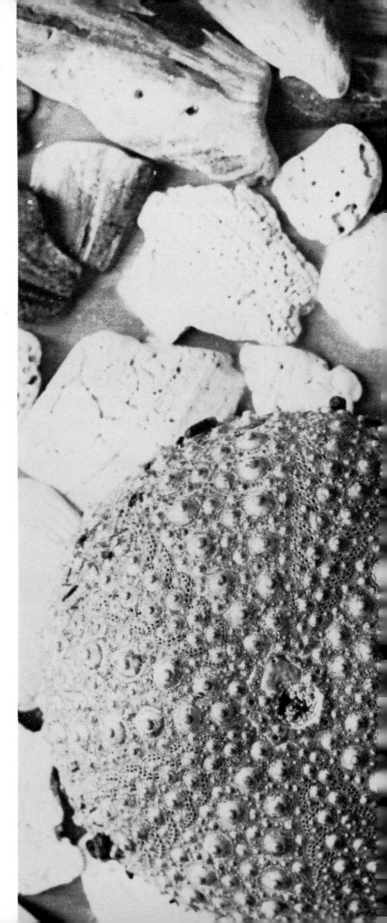

direct or *indirect* method. But there are many other techniques you may wish to try — found objects, assemblages, constructions, to name a few — as well as those more allied to the traditional methods.

This book was not intended as a *complete* book of instruction to include all the infinite ramifications of techniques employed by various artists. No single volume of this length would be able to embrace that amount of information. But there *is* sufficient basic instruction in *Modern Mosaic Techniques* for the beginner to approach his project in an intelligent, professional manner.

Many of the projects illustrated were made especially for this book and are reproduced here for the first time. The book was designed to inspire the reader, to give him an insight into the endless possibilities of producing decorative surfaces, as well as to provide some basic instruction.

For both the newcomer and the professional, it is hoped that what he sees on these pages will encourage him to begin to produce some interesting mosaics, perhaps even to create new and exciting techniques of his own.

FOUND OBJECT MOSAIC *(detail) by Janice Greenberg, made from shells, fragmented rocks and pebbles, and sea urchins.*

2. INDIRECT METHOD

Until about twenty-five years ago, most of the mosaics done in the United States were murals or architectural decorations. These were commissioned works usually designed by an artist, often one who had never done a mosaic before, and executed by craftsmen in one of the five or six large professional mosaic shops that existed in this country at that time. The artist seldom worked directly on the mosaic.

After the mid-forties, the art of mosaic began to attract creative artists and craftsmen as a vehicle for direct expression. By the mid-fifties, mosaic had become generally so popular, and the techniques had been so simplified through the development of new tesserae and adhesives, that there were even do-it-yourself mosaic kits on the market for the layman.

This book discusses primarily the new, simplified techniques. However, it is good for anyone who makes mosaics to have an acquaintance with the traditional technique that has been practiced by mosaic artists and craftsmen (almost unchanged) for more than 1500 years. Many of the techniques used by artists today are variations and simplifications of this technique.

TRADITIONAL MURAL TECHNIQUE

The following are the steps in the design and execution of a large mural, done by, or with the

In a professional mosaic shop — Venetian Art Mosaics, Inc., in New York City — the floor is covered with sections of a mosaic done by the indirect technique. In the foreground are sections of a cartoon, partially covered with tesserae. In the center of the photo, a color sketch of the mosaic design is hung for reference as the tiles are laid. Along the walls in the background, the tiles are stored in shallow containers.

aid of, assistants. Small mosaic panels may be done by the same technique, in simplified form, as demonstrated later in this chapter.

The artist first completes his preliminary and presentation sketches and selects the basic colors of tesserae. His proposal is presented to the architect and the client. Upon approval of the sketches, the final contract is drawn, which gives the artist authority to proceed on the actual mosaic work, plus funds with which to pay for the progress on the work.

The artist may either hire skilled craftsmen as assistants to work in his studio, or he may sub-contract the work to a professional mosaic shop. In the areas where the building trades unions are strong, he will be subjected to great pressure to sub-contract the job to a professional union mosaic shop.

COLOR SKETCH AND LINE CARTOON

The presentation sketch will usually suffice as a color working sketch — if one is not too disturbed by the necessity of viewing it in a mirror while working, since the tesserae are laid in *reverse*. On large works, time will be saved, and the chance of error greatly reduced, by making an enlarged color sketch the *reverse* of the presentation sketch. This becomes even more important as the number of assistants is expanded.

A full-scale line cartoon is made on a 90 lb. press brown paper. This cartoon must be the reverse of the presentation sketch — a mirror image of it — enlarged. The paper upon which the cartoon is drawn comes in wide rolls. On murals that exceed the width of the available roll of paper, the paper is taped together from behind with masking tape to make a *single* sheet of paper the size of the mural.

PASTING THE TESSERAE

If the artist has no experience in actually pasting the tesserae and setting the mosaic sections into the cement, he should, at this point, confer with the foreman of the mosaic shop to see if any lines should be changed for technical reasons; he should also get advice on the best places to cut the sections to facilitate mounting the mosaic in the cement.

These sections should be about three square feet in area. With a wide marking felt (using a color other than that which was used to draw the cartoon), the cut lines are diagrammed on the cartoon. With a mat knife or other sharp pointed blade, the sections are cut apart along the center of the cut lines. Each section is then numbered in sequence, beginning on the *back* of the section in the lower right corner, working across the backs of the bottom row of sections, then moving up to the next row.

Each assistant is given a section at a time to work on — paste up the tesserae on brown paper. If the original presentation sketch is referred to by the assistants for color guidance, it is always referred to *through a mirror*. On large murals, it is always worth the extra time for the artist to make a large color cartoon the reverse of the original sketch; in the long run, it saves work time and minimizes chances for errors. The artist supervises carefully to see that the color mixes and the spacing of tesserae by the various assistants remain consistent.

The glue that is used to paste the tesserae to the paper is an ancient formula of gum arabic, flour, and blackstrap (or crude) molasses. The recipe for this glue is given in Chapter 1. The section of brown paper that is being worked on is entirely coated with the glue, applied with a brush. The tesserae are set right into this bed of glue, just as they are taken from their storage containers. The colors of tesserae that are to be used on a particular section are picked by the artist and placed in shallow containers. The assistants place these containers conveniently at the edges of the sections that they are working on. Cutting tools are at hand for each assistant; these are the hutch and scaling hammer, cutting tools described in Chapter 1.

As various sections are pasted, they are assembled in a jigsaw puzzle on the floor. After the entire mosaic has been assembled, it is carefully studied by the artist for any revisions that may be desired. This is the last stage when revisions may be made without inordinate effort. *Ideally*, the artist should have a balcony about 15' above the floor from which to view the assembled mosaic; but for those not so fortunate, a tall ladder and a reducing glass will do. The mosaic is examined in the mirror to see how the installed work will look.

If the artist is completely satisfied with the color and composition, then the joints of the sections are checked to see if the lines of the tesserae — in adjoining planes between sections — seem to flow together smoothly, and to see that there is no apparent variation in the color or rhythm of the lines of the tesserae.

INSTALLATION

The sections are then stacked — beginning in the upper right corner — one row at a time. Thus, the upper right corner is on the bottom of the pile and the upper left corner is on the top of the stack.

The sections are delivered to the site and placed in a protected area near the wall upon which the mosaic will be set. This wall is prepared with a brown coat of stucco cement, with a scratch finish, by the masons of the general contractor.

The installation work must begin early in the morning to assure eight hours of uninterrupted work. On a large job, a cement mixer is essential. The proportions of cement and aggregate are given in Chapter 1. Beginning in the lower left corner, the wall is thoroughly wetted down for

an area of about fifty square feet. Then, with a plasterer's or mason's trowel, cement is applied about ½″ thick over an area large enough to receive the first four or five paper sections — about twenty square feet laterally across the bottom of the wall.

A thin layer of the cement mix is applied directly to the mosaic (on the brown paper) with the trowel; this is called *buttering* the mosaic section. The buttered side of the section is set into the cement on the wall so that the tiles are set into the wet cement. Then, with a hammer and a wide board, the section is tamped firmly into place. The job proceeds laterally in this manner across the bottom of the wall, until the bottom row is set, and continues in numbered order with the next row and the next.

At the end of three hours, or about noon, the workers stop for lunch. During this time, the last sections that were set have time to dry. After lunch, the workers wet the brown paper on all of the sections that were set in the morning. The paper turns quite dark and the impressions of the tesserae will be seen through the back of the paper. Warm water will expedite this stage of the work. After about fifteen minutes of soaking, the paper is peeled off, beginning with the top of the *first* section that was set and working across in the same order that they are numbered. (Always peel a section *from the top* and with great care.)

When the paper is removed, the surface of the tesserae will have a residue of the brown glue. This is removed by washing with a wet sponge. When all of the glue is removed, the mosaic area should be tamped again, care being given to close up all the gaps between the sections by gently pushing the tesserae together where gaps exist. The cement from underneath the tesserae will be forced up between the cracks during the tamping process, thus providing the grout. When the surface is level, more cement from the first mix may be rubbed into the cracks that still exist. Finally, the whole area is washed again with a wet sponge.

Before quitting for the day, if the installation has not been completed, any exposed cement — where tile has not yet been applied — must be removed down to the scratch finish so that work can begin the next day directly on the brown stucco coat.

After the mosaic is completely installed, a day is allowed for the last installed sections to set. Then the entire mosaic is washed down with muriatic acid, full strength. Goggles, gloves, a cap, and protective clothing are worn. Immediately upon completion of the acid application, the mosaic should be washed down with a soda and water solution. Then comes a final rinse of clear water. The finished mosaic is dried and polished with crumpled old newspapers.

DEMONSTRATION OF INDIRECT TECHNIQUE

Naturally, artists develop their own variations in technique. Smaller works afford far more possibilities for variation and simplification. Victor Casados explains his procedure in his description of the design and execution of his 24″ x 36″ mosaic panel, *Birds*, created especially for this book by the indirect method.

"I first make thumbnail sketches — lots of them! I then select the most promising designs and refine them. Then I make various small color roughs. After selecting the best color schemes, I make at least two color comprehensives, refining the designs as I go."

PRELIMINARY DRAWINGS

Two color comprehensives of *Birds* were first made to scale, rendered in designer's colors. One was a cool scheme; the other utilized shades of pale yellow to very bright yellow, yellow-browns,

rusty red, Wedgewood blue, orange tones, and off white. The latter scheme was selected because of its richness.

The next step was to make a full-size drawing — or cartoon — of the bird design. This was done on tracing paper with charcoal, so that necessary adjustments in shapes, values, etc., could be easily made. "Then I place the tracing paper *face down* on a piece of heavy brown wrapping paper (90 lb. press is the best). I trace the *outline* of my design on the back of the transparent tracing paper, thus transferring the charcoal to the brown paper. By doing this, I obtain the *reverse image* of my design on the brown paper."

It is on this brown paper cartoon that the tesserae will be laid.

APPLYING TESSERAE

To set the tesserae on the paper cartoon requires a mixture that will hold it fast, yet not be permanent. To make such a solution, you will need equal parts of blackstrap molasses and rye flour. Here is the way Casados prepares it:

First, mix the flour with water, just enough to make a smooth paste — as you would mix gravy. Then mix this flour paste with the molasses and place it over a low heat. Stir the mixture constantly to keep lumps from forming, and keep it *below the boiling point*. Mix just enough to use during the time you will be working because the paste spoils within a week. Since the paste is so easy to prepare, it is best to mix it as you need it.

Brush this glue mixture over the entire surface of the brown paper onto which the cartoon has been transferred. By covering the entire surface with the glue at once, you will minimize buckling of the paper. Then begin to apply the tesserae directly into the glue, beginning at a logical place in relation to your sketch. (You can also *butter* each tile with glue and set it on the dry paper.) It is advisable to place the perimeter tesserae as early as is convenient, so you can avoid having to place halved and quartered pieces along the edges.

Casados' color sketch was used as a guide, but he felt free to change his mind as the pattern developed — when change improved the design. "There's so much going on in a mosaic," he explains, "I am open to change until the panel is finally grouted." One of the purposes of the *indirect* method is to allow the artist to change and improve his design as much as he desires. In the *direct* method, you have to chip the tile out to make a change. In the *indirect* method, it's only a matter of dampening the paper a little and pulling your tile off.

Here are a few basic ideas which the artist suggests to help you in setting your designs:

"Try creating different directions with the tile as you work, always keeping the movement of the pattern in mind. If you cut tiles, try to keep the cuts simple (such as cutting a tile directly in half or making a straight diagonal cut through the tile, rather than cutting small pieces). The fewer the cuts, the better, and keep them within an area of the design, rather than along the edges.

"It is better to use uncut pieces where one form in your design meets another shape; this helps to *define* your forms. Try to create interest within an area. Try unusual notes of color here and there."

In his panel, *Birds*, Casados has sparingly used pieces of bright royal blue, bright yellow-green, and orange-red. Using both Venetian and Byzantine tesserae, he has created surface interest, since one type (Venetian) is flat and even, and the other (Byzantine) is uneven in size and of different depths. To get a better perspective of the overall design, a reducing glass was used. "You can't put your mosaic upright as you work — the reducing glass gives the effect of how the pieces will look at a distance."

PREPARING PANEL

To prepare the panel into which the tesserae were to be *finally set in reverse*, a 1″ plywood board was selected. Heavy board is best because it is less inclined to warp. Casados sealed the wood with a commercial sealer, using a 2″ house painter's brush, brushing first in one direction, then in the other. It is very important that the wood be sealed because moisture can cause warping.

After sealing, the panel was set aside and allowed to *dry thoroughly* before the next step was attempted.

TRANSFERRING TESSERAE TO PANEL

When the panel was completely dry, the setting of the tesserae was done in mastic. This material comes already prepared; it is light weight and easy to handle.

The mastic was applied to the panel with a trowel. To make the panel dry faster, the mastic was *combed* with a saw-tooth trowel, whose tooth-like prongs create a slightly uneven surface. *Combing* also helps the tesserae stay in place, and keeps the mastic from seeping up on the sides. The board with mastic coating was then put aside for about ten minutes to allow the mastic to partially set.

Next the panel was held directly above the mosaic tesserae — mastic side facing the surface of the tesserae — and carefully lowered onto the surface of the tesserae, with attention being given to the correct alignment of the edges and corners. Then the panel was pressed firmly into the mosaic. It is important that the tesserae be pressed firmly into the mastic covered board. Casados presses down with both feet on *both sides* — the board side and the paper side. (This method presents certain technical difficulties if tesserae of uneven thickness are used; the varying thickness of the Venetian glass tiles and the smalti makes it difficult to get the thinner tesserae properly imbedded in the mastic. It is easier when only Venetian glass tiles are used in the mosaic.)

The panel is then put aside for a few minutes to permit the mastic to set further so that the tesserae will not come loose when they are cleaned. Then, with water and a sponge, the paper is soaked thoroughly until you can see the outline of the design come through.

When you remove the paper from the panel, the paper should be pulled *toward you*; there is less tendency to pull up tesserae along with the paper, if you do it this way. Pull up part of the paper and expose *one edge* of the finished panel first, just to be sure that the tesserae have been set firmly in place. Be careful, when you clean the tesserae, not to lift off any tiles.

GROUTING AND CLEANING

This panel was grouted, using prepared grout mixed with grout color to obtain a rich brown.

To clean tesserae, water and a sponge are used. But to remove the film left by the grout, Casados cleaned the panel with one part hydrochloric (muriatic) acid to six parts water. ("Be sure to wear gloves when using this solution," he warns.) This solution not only cleans the tiles but makes them sparkle. The mosaic should then be washed with a solution of two tablespoons of baking soda dissolved in a pint of water, followed by a clear water rinse.

Polishing should then be done with a clean, soft, dry rag. A final polishing with crumpled old newspapers will heighten the luster of the tesserae because of the polishing action of the silicone in paper. The final step is to fit the mosaic panel into a wooden frame.

Victor Casados chooses a semi-abstract manner of working out his design, Birds. In this watercolor sketch, he is careful to emphasize dark and light values so that the design will be well defined when translated into terms of tesserae.

A pen and ink line drawing accentuates the outline and general rhythm of his design. A smaller color sketch is referred to as he works, but his idea of the color scheme is well worked out in his mind, also. Here he is shown laying tesserae on a sketch made on brown paper. Each tessera is buttered with a small palette knife and glued to the paper surface with a mixture of molasses and rye flour, mixed to a syrupy consistency. Tesserae colors are separated and placed in individual bottles.

Two coats of sealer are used as a protective finish on the board before any work is started. This must be thoroughly dried before mastic is applied. A 2" house painter's brush is used for brushing sealer onto a 1" board. (Step 1)

Mastic is spread with a trowel over the plywood board after the sealer is completely dry. (Step 2)

To dry the mastic quickly, a tooth-edged implement is combed through the wet material. (Step 3)

The mastic-coated board is lowered over the mosaic, which has been set on the paper cartoon. It is best for two persons to handle this step, to make sure that the tesserae are pressed into the mastic solidly and accurately. (Step 4)

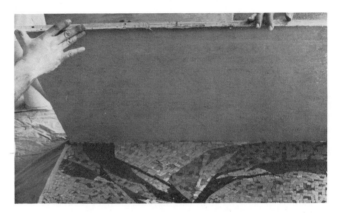

Feet are used to press the board and paper (with the mosaic design on it) together solidly. Feet are pressed down on both sides of the mosaic — the board side and the paper side. (Step 5)

The paper is soaked with water and rubbed over with a sponge until you can see the outline of the mosaic design underneath. Then one corner is cautiously raised; care must be taken not to loosen the tesserae. (Step 6)

Detail of Victor Casados' Birds

Completed mosaic panel, Birds, by Victor Casados. This piece was done by the indirect method. The movement in the design gives the feeling of flight in the bird forms.

SUMMER FLOWERS by Harriet Lane, indirect method. Harriet Lane often finds flowers inspiring as subject matter for panels executed in the indirect technique. She begins by working out her ideas in a more or less abstract way, using paper collage, water base paints, oils, or synthetics on either Masonite or board. Occasionally, she further explores a first sketch by making a completed abstract painting of her subject. Then she traces the original design on transparent tracing paper. She then turns the paper over — reverses it — and outlines the design on the opposite side of the tracing paper. Because the paper is transparent, the design is easy to follow. Following the procedure outlined in this chapter, she places the tesserae on the paper with a mixture of rye flour and molasses. When the design is completed, the entire thing is reversed onto a previously prepared board which has builder's wire stretched over it and cement or magnesite poured over the wire screen mesh. In this vertical panel, the light tones of the flowers weave a pattern through the deep, richly colored background.

SUMMER THISTLES by Dextra Frankel, indirect method. This artist's ideas often spring from nature and she treats these themes in an original, stylized manner. The panel is 19" x 30".

44

3. DIRECT METHOD

In this method of making a mosaic, each piece of material is either set directly into the adhesive or embedded in mortar. Because there are endless variations of the *direct technique*, the selections of materials, glues, mortar, and the like must be determined by the artist's design and his individual manner of working *directly*. Instead of Byzantine or Venetian tesserae, he may choose anything from bleached bones to pieces of a discarded wrist watch. What he chooses must obviously be practical for his purpose. A steadily increasing number of craftsmen are finding the *direct technique* an exciting one. Some feel it has an advantage due to the fact that they can *see what they are doing* because the tiles are right side up. Interesting effects can be achieved by tilting or slanting the tesserae; but in order to set them firmly, mastic or mortar must be used.

In this chapter the works of a number of artists who use the direct method are set forth, each differing from the other in design concept and working methods.

REQUIREMENTS OF PROJECT

This commission called for a mosaic pattern to be set on the hood over an electric kitchen stove in the home of Mr. and Mrs. Joseph Mitchell in Beverly Hills. The task was an unusual one, providing a challenging project in the *direct tech-*

BATHROOM TILE ABSTRACTION by Allen Garrett, direct method. Here is an original and interesting variation of the direct method, made with ordinary bathroom tile mounted on a wooden panel.

nique for artist Kayla Salzer. This job is indicative of a trend toward using mosaics in the home, as an integral part of the design of a room.

The plywood panels over the stove hood faced two different views of the kitchen. One, over the electric grill, looked out to an open patio. The other looked into the large working area of the kitchen. These panels were intended to hold the mosaic design.

In addition to the mosaic on the hood, tiles had to be designed and made by hand for the working area just below the wood. These were planned as ceramic tiles, hand decorated to tie in with the other kitchen decor. Both the mosaics and the tiles shown in the step-by-step illustrations were designed and executed by Miss Salzer, who is a painter and sculptress as well as a mosaicist.

PRELIMINARY SKETCH

A preliminary sketch, drawn to scale, was rendered in watercolor. Sometimes this artist's sketches materialize in the form of a collage. On a commissioned job, a sketch of some kind is usually mandatory. The purpose of a rough sketch is to establish the principal areas of the design, rather than the detail. The colors here also suggested a general scheme — not a precise one — and roughly indicate handmade tiles to be set below the panel.

EXECUTING THE DESIGN

Working directly on a plywood panel attached to the wall, the artist lightly sketched in the design with a pencil.

When the sketch on the plywood was finished, wire screen mesh was stretched over the board and nailed down to reinforce the cement where the tesserae were to be set. Several pairs of clippers, putty knives, and a small trowel were the only implements used.

Using the pencil lines as a guide, the artist filled small areas with plaster cement, working with the small trowel. Only a few inches may be worked on at a time because the cement dries rapidly. (Plaster cement was Miss Salzer's choice for this mosaic, but an extended working time, desirable under most circumstances, may be achieved by using a cement, lime, and sand mix as described in Chapter 1. White cement may be substituted for the Portland cement if a white setting bed is desired.) The cement was spread thickly and unevenly, since the desired effect was not a smooth surface.

Each tessera was cut with tin snips — varying them in size and shape to fit individual small areas of design — as the artist worked. Each tessera was tipped or tilted in the wet cement. This artist *never* sets tesserae so as to appear completely flat: "I like to think of setting tesserae as though I were painting — each one is a brush stroke."

You will observe that the spaces between the tesserae are not symmetrical in shape or size. Some of them are as wide as the tesserae themselves. This was done deliberately to avoid a stiff, "set" appearance.

COLOR AND TEXTURE

The design was inspired by nature, with the sun as the central motif. Clear shades of yellow, mustard, pink, lavender, green, and white were used in the butterflies, sun rays, leaves, and other details.

To add sparkle and to accentuate the sun theme, many pieces of shining gold tesserae were incorporated into the design. These gold tesserae were placed *first*, establishing a glittering pattern flowing through the panel — like a gold thread woven through a tapestry. Then the rest of the colors were placed in juxtaposition to the gold.

Textures were constantly varied by moving the tesserae about.

Kayla Salzer prefers to work spontaneously. "The design and the color are always subject to change. The detail changes from day to day as I work on each section. I'm more concerned with texture and color than with following a design exactly. I like to leave myself free."

It is this freedom, incorporated into her designs, that gives them originality and a great deal of charm.

Preliminary sketch of kitchen mural by artist Kayla Salzer. The sketch shows the general scheme of the mural panel, as well as that of the handmade tiles to be set directly below.

Each piece of tesserae is cut with a clipper to a variety of shapes and sizes as the work progresses. Discarded plastic and tin food containers are used to hold the tesserae.

With a small trowel, plastic cement is spread unevenly over the wire screen mesh, previously nailed to the plywood panel. The design has been pencilled in lightly on the plywood underneath the wire. Only a small area is covered at one time because the cement dries rapidly.

When the cement is spread over a small area, the artist places the tesserae in position, tipping or tilting them in the cement.

Completed mosaic-covered stove
hood, with handmade ceramic tiles
below. This panel faces an outdoor
patio.

Detail of sun motif. Notice the various
shapes and sizes of tesserae. ▶

WOMAN by Kayla Salzer, direct technique. Whatever the subject, Kayla Salzer attacks it in a bold, original manner. Here she has used fragments of broken glass and mirrored bits, with the dark hair and the outline of the arms and figure as strong accents.

OWL by Janice Lovoos, direct technique. This richly textured panel was made from fragments of broken white china, beer bottles, and soft drink bottles, combined with tesserae and marble dust in the background. ▶

MOSAIC MURAL by Glen Michaels,
direct technique. Here Glen Michaels
is at work on a mural made of wooden
pieces and tile in the Chase Hotel,
St. Louis, Missouri. Size 32' x 10'.

4. SANDCASTING

Sandcasting combines features of both the *indirect* and *direct* mosaic techniques: the tesserae are set directly into the sand and the design is in reverse when finished. Ever since Robert Seyle introduced this method at Otis Art Institute several years ago, other students have found it a simple and effective way of working.

In the example illustrated, the *Buffalo* sketch was first rendered in watercolor by artist, Robert Seyle, who also executed the design.

PLACING TESSERAE IN BOX

A wooden frame the exact size of the sketch is constructed of boards and put together loosely because this makes the finished mosaic easier to remove. A bottom is added.

Sand is then poured into the frame, entirely covering the bottom. The sand, poured to 1" thickness, is smoothed over with a flat, squeegee-like board.

Next, the preliminary sketch is placed on the table alongside the sand filled box for reference. The artist lightly sketches a comparable design in the sand, using a pencil point. Selecting colors at will, he sets each tile separately, taking liberties with the original scheme (which carries little or no detail). A few small areas are left; in these areas, delicate scrolls are incised with a pencil point in the sand.

MOSAIC CROSS by Joe Elliot, sandcasting method. Because he used ordinary bathroom (ceramic) tile in soft rose, beige, brown, off-white, and gray — all closely related in tone — the artist obtained some of the contrast from the way in which the tiles were set. Notice how he cut oblong, square, and diamond shapes of varying sizes, setting them face forward or crosswise, slanting them or angling them in all directions.

The edge of a thin piece of cardboard is used to guide Byzantine and Venetian tesserae into place and to separate them. Then the tesserae are rearranged until the design is satisfactory to the artist.

POURING MAGNESITE OVER TESSERAE

Next, magnesite is mixed with magnesium chloride to the consistency of a thick cake batter in a medium sized plastic bowl. If the mixture is too thin, it loses its strength as a binding agent.

When thoroughly mixed, the magnesite mixture is poured over the tesserae and spread evenly with a palette knife or a flat stick. The magnesite should be almost floated on so that the arrangement of tesserae underneath is not disturbed. Pouring the magnesite over one small area at a time makes the thick liquid easier to handle. It should be at least ½" thick. But easy does it! Cement and hydrocal may also be used — in place of the magnesite — in making sandcastings.

When the panel is completely covered, builders cloth — a heavy screen mesh used in construction — is gently pressed into the magnesite with the forefinger until the mixture oozes up over the wire screen and the screen is completely obscured. This mesh is used to reinforce the layer of magnesite. This step, and pouring the magnesite, should be done an hour or two before the mosaic starts to set.

SEPARATING PANEL FROM BOX

Before the panel is set aside, a hammer is tapped around the edges of the frame to make certain that the magnesite has settled into place. A palette knife is used to skim around the edges to keep the magnesite from sticking when the panel is later removed. It's the same principle used to keep a cake from sticking to the pan.

This panel is allowed to stand for eight hours before the next step is attempted. The setting of tesserae should never be rushed. If they are not thoroughly set, the edges of the tesserae are likely to break off when the panel is removed.

The frame is pulled apart with a chisel and hammer; the finished panel is lifted out with sand clinging to its edges. These granules and other loose particles are brushed off with a bristle brush. Then the rough outside edges are squared off with a hammer and chisel.

Because this artist prefers deep color and a dull finish, all the colors — blue, green, off-white, orange, and bright brown — are toned down with a stain of oil color blended with turpentine. The surplus is then wiped off with a soft rag, producing an effect of subtle, rich coloring.

A frame — sides and bottom — is loosely constructed with boards, nails, and carpenter's hammer so the panel can be easily removed when completed.

Ordinary sand is poured into the frame, about ¼″ deep.

The surface of the sand is smoothed over with a piece of board.

Following the sketch placed alongside the frame, the artist draws the design in the sand lightly with a pencil. He is now ready to place the tesserae.

Here is the original watercolor sketch; below it is the design drawn in the sand.

The artist begins to set the tesserae, starting with the darkest tone, which in this case is black. He separates the pieces with the point of a thin piece of cardboard.

The design finished, he begins to pour the magnesite over the entire panel.

He pushes the magnesite onto the panel with a stick, being careful not to disturb the tesserae arrangement. The adhesive is floated gently over the material so as not to spoil the design.

Builders' cloth (also called hardware cloth), a screen mesh used in construction, is placed over the magnesite. Pressing with the forefinger, the artist gently pushes the mesh down until it is completely obscured. Builders' cloth is used solely to reinforce the magnesite.

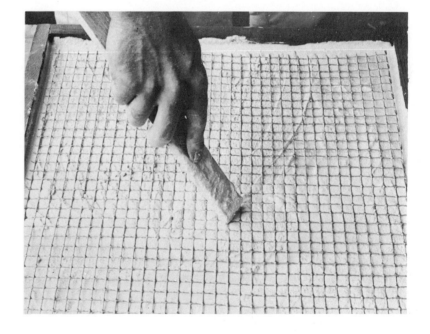

After the magnesite has set, the frame is knocked away from the panel with hammer and chisel. Here is the way the panel looks prior to cleaning off the sand. This is the back of the panel.

Standing the panel on end, he brushes away the surplus sand and other loose particles with a bristle brush. Notice the impression of the design left in the sand.

To tone down the color, an oil and turpentine stain is washed over the panel with a painter's brush, then wiped away. This stain is used on the entire area, including the black and brown tesserae.

The finished mosaic. You will notice
that the design is the reverse of the
original sketch.

66

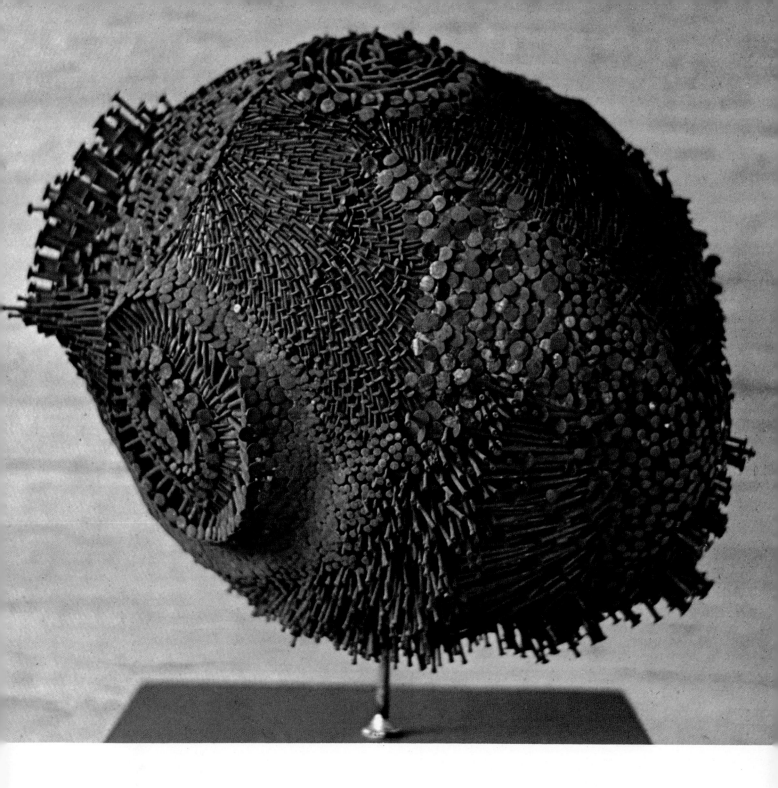

NAIL MOSAIC SCULPTURE by Robert Seyle. Nails were hammered into a wooden core and the entire form re- volves on a motor driven shaft. Note how the nails run in different direc- tions, producing a lively surface flow.

PASTA MOSAIC SCULPTURES by Helen Luitjens. Various shapes of macaroni were cemented to a styrofoam (foam plastic) core with a commercial white glue, which dries clear and invisible. The sculpture was sprayed with white, matte enamel, then lightly sprayed with additional colors which allow the white to glow through.

MINARETS by Dextra Frankel. Made by the indirect technique, this decorative panel combines rectangular and triangular tesserae. Note how the placement of the tesserae often follows the shapes of the architecture, particularly the curving domes of the mosques. ▶

PASTA PANEL by Helen Luitjens. Various shapes and sizes of macaroni were cemented to a 12" x 12" styrofoam square. The panel was first sprayed with white, matte enamel; then lightly sprayed with green, followed by gold, applied from the side so that no heavy spray covers any area. The final finish was a clear acrylic spray.

◀

CRATERS '66 by David Partridge, nail mosaic. Grouped in interlocking circles that actually form "craters," the nails also produce a rich pattern that exploits the various metallic finishes in which nails are manufactured. This panel was designed as a ceiling for an entrance hall.

71

◄ STAINED GLASS MOSAIC by Jack Stewart. In this modern version of an ancient art form, the artist has eliminated the traditional lead mullions which normally bind the glass segments. Stained glass is cut or broken into mosaic tesserae size, then laminated with epoxy resin to a sheet of plate glass. Such stained glass panels are impervious to weather.

SPRUCE GROUSE by Emile Norman, inlaid woods and epoxy resins, 15" high. The artist first models his forms in wax, over which a shell of wood inlay and epoxy is constructed. The wax is then melted out, leaving a hollow figure.

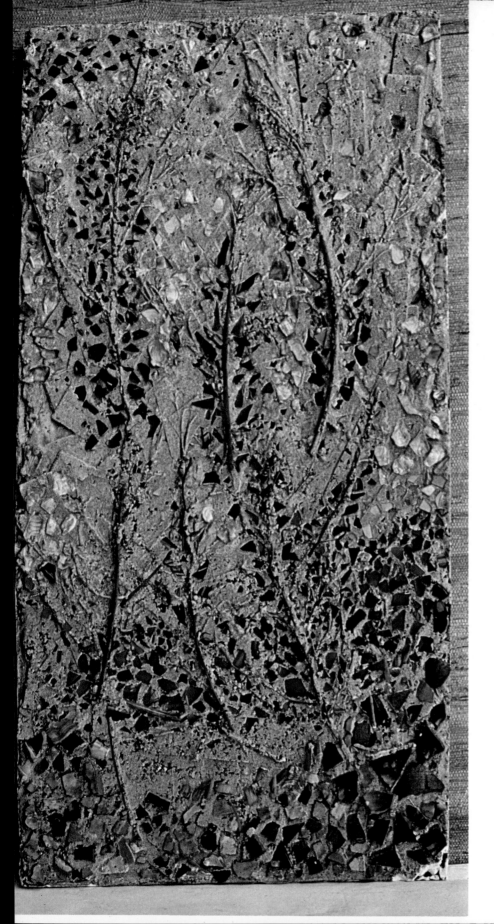

LEAF DESIGN by Janice Woolett, sandcasting. This delicately colored panel combines the texture of the sand with colored glass fragments which surround stem-like shapes in relief.

DIANA by Jack Stewart, sandcasting, 20" x 30". A bed of wet sand (in a 20" x 30" wooden box) was carved in relief. Then tesserae and crushed marble were inserted into certain areas of the composition, leaving the sand untouched in other areas. A fluid mixture of hydrocal was gently poured over the surface to a depth of ½". Hardware cloth was placed over the wet hydrocal and another ½" layer of hydrocal was poured over the metal mesh. When the hydrocal had set, the box was broken away from the mosaic panel and the excess sand dusted from the surface of the hydrocal, leaving a thin layer of sand adhering to the hydrocal around the tesserae.

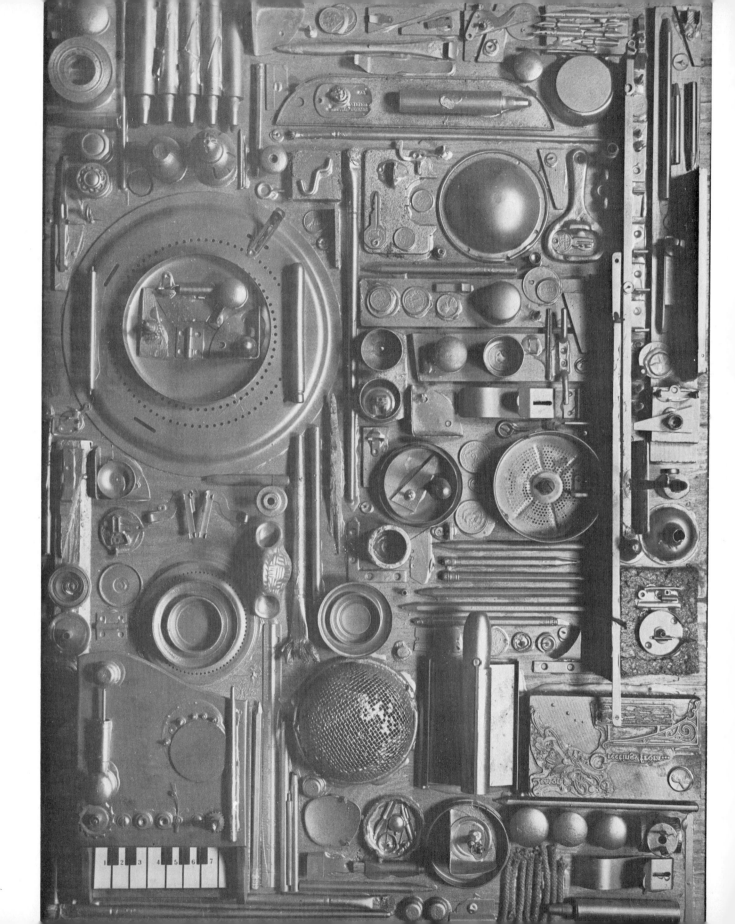

5. FOUND OBJECTS

Unique mosaics may be made by assembling materials that are roughly classified as *found objects*. These can include bits of broken china or glass, fragments of wood, metal stampings, rusty keys, hinges, parts of old motors — in short, anything salvaged from junkyards or other places where discards are to be found.

Start a found objects mosaic by first considering the true worth of your material as a creative medium, *not as junk per se*. Their tactile qualities often have immediate appeal; they may offer endless means for producing fascinating textures and surfaces. The subtle colors and great variety of shapes and sizes will stimulate design ideas.

This is basically a *direct method* of working, one that challenges the imagination and begs you to be flexible in your approach so that you may change your design — even your entire concept — as you work.

EXPERIMENTING WITH THE DESIGN ELEMENTS

After gathering the materials, begin by placing them on a board of plywood and pushing them about until you arrive at some sort of general pattern. Found objects usually possess intrinsic esthetic values suited to abstractions because the materials themselves offer so much excitement in texture and form. If you wish, draw in your

MUSIC MACHINE #1 by Arthur Secunda, 34" high. Carefully chosen discards from the kitchen, worn-out paint brushes, parts of machinery, and an amazing collection of other "junk" take on a new dimension when coated with polyester resin and tinted green-gold. Collection, Manning Post, Beverly Hills.

design lightly with a pencil to serve as a guide.

Keep moving the objects around, eliminating anything that is distracting or unpleasing to the eye, or that *does not add to the design as a whole.* Add any new items that you feel are necessary and place the objects so that they complement one another in color, texture, and spatial organization. The over-all design should have a feeling of rhythm. Arrange the color and value contrasts so that, when seen at a distance, there is a clear separation between the forms. Work with the design until it has a feeling of movement and until the gradation of color, texture, light, and dark are also pleasing.

When you are completely satisfied with your arrangement, start carefully gluing each piece into place. There are special adhesives for working with glass, metal, wood, or whatever the material may be. A hobby shop or hardware store can advise you about the appropriate adhesive. Found objects may also be embedded in grout.

FOUND OBJECTS FROM NATURE

Nature is a storehouse of treasures for the artist-craftsman. He can explore the beaches, mountain creeks, streams, and river beds for his materials. Many of them may be effectively used for mosaic and other techniques in creations that range from ashtrays to a stepping stone walk for the garden or an inset for the patio floor.

If one lives near the ocean — or relatively close — it is well worth a day's trip to come home with a sackful of pebbles, sea shells, and interesting fragments.

Natural materials may also be combined with man-made found objects — metal, wood, glass, etc., set in cement — on wood panels. You can combine fish skeletons, seaweed, bits of broken glass, or wire — the sky's the limit!

Go hunting in your favorite outdoor haunt. You may be surprised at the materials that have always been there, just waiting for you to use them.

EXAMPLES IN THIS CHAPTER

Illustrated in this chapter are found objects, mosaics, and panels made by a group of artists with varying backgrounds. Some pieces were executed by professional mosaicists and craftsmen on an elaborate scale. Often pieces were executed by artists already established in fine arts fields — painters and sculptors.

Whatever your status as an artist or craftsman, if you enjoy being a scavenger and like to turn discards into something unique, whimsical, handsome, found objects mosaics will give you a lively creative outlet.

E SQUARED by Chris Lemon, *wooden found objects.* Out of your environment may come ideas for your work in mosaic techniques. Chris Lemon's husband is a builder and it was on the floor of his workshop that she found the materials which she has combined so delightfully in her found objects panels. Made primarily from an assortment of wooden fragments and chips, these panels also utilize bits of broken screen wire, wooden dowels, and twine. Whereas much of the wood is left in its natural state, she sometimes paints pieces white, a bright color, or deeper brown tones for accents or to strengthen the overall design. In E Squared, she has combined natural wood and painted wooden pieces. The E was cut out with a coping saw and painted a deep blue. Directly above it is another square, the wooden top of a discarded plastic container. The wooden pieces are arranged around the edges to form part of the casual framing that holds the design together.

PANEL by Chris Lemon, wooden
found objects with string and screen-
ing. Two-by-fours divide and bisect
this found objects panel. Wooden
dowels, wrapping twine, white push
pins, and wire mesh add interest.

80

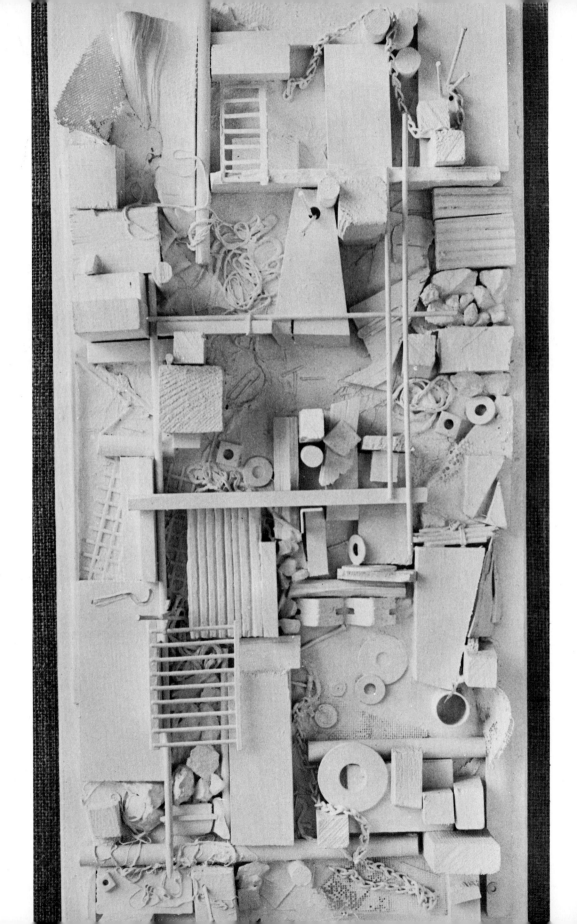

PANEL by Arthur Secunda. This artist's preference for heavy textures, seen in his paintings, is reflected in assemblages made from parts of discarded sewing machines, cars, lamps and lamp bases, light fuses, keys, and wood turnings, among numerous other items, all strung together with heavy wire pieces and held fast with coats of polyester resin. A finish of gold or gold-green gives them a rich color that also helps to unify these designs of many diverse parts.

Texture predominates in this panel created from junk. In a pleasing arrangement, the artist has combined the most unlikely pieces; discarded metalware, old paint brushes, wood fragments, a golf ball, etc. Coated in its entirety with polyester resin, the piece was given a coating of gold-green which gives it a metallic cast.

WHARFSIDE #1 by Chris Lemon, wooden found objects, string, and metal waste. This tall, narrow wooden panel, white on white, combines a potpourri of items other than wood bits and pieces. Metal rings, nuts and bolts, twine, nails, wire mesh, pieces cut from plastic strawberry boxes, and pieces of metal chain are all glued to the plywood board with epoxy resin. The entire thing is sprayed a rich, creamy white.

◀

SEASHELL PANEL by Janice Greenberg, found objects mosaic. This artist frequently takes trips to investigate tide pools and their yield of waterwashed materials. This interest began when she made a series of cardboard panels filled with seashells to raise funds for the Boy Scouts. Some of the found treasures she works with are fragments of scallop shells, rocks eaten away by water and time, crab legs, abalone fragments, fish skeletons, fish jaws, blue mussel shells, sea anemones, whelks, sea urchins — all acquired on public beaches. Sometimes she adds bits of black glass, or small pieces of seaweed, etc. for variation.

Working on a plywood board, she fastens each piece carefully with white glue (polyvinyl acetate). A study of this artist's work shows how selectively she chooses and combines materials. Note the interesting juxtaposition of varied sizes and shapes. When materials are heavily textured (such as sea urchin shells), fewer materials of different kinds are combined. When many small pieces are joined to make a panel, the artist makes certain that a strong design holds them together. Time, therefore, must be allowed for the artist to rearrange and reshuffle the pieces before setting them with glue, so that the over-all effect will be good.

After the artist has planned out what effect she wants in her panel, she starts gluing the elements into place on the plywood.

DECORATIVE PANEL by Janice Greenberg, made from pebbles, shell fragments, bits of seaweed, sea urchins, sea anenomes. Notice how strong values of dark, light, and medium tones are established by skillful placement of shell fragments, tiny shells, pebbles, sea urchins, bits of kelp and seaweed, thus producing a definite over-all pattern.

MOSAIC BOX by John Smith. A plywood box is covered with black, white, and gray pebbles from Mexico, using a simple bird motif as the cover design. The pebbles were fastened to the wood surface with Wilhold glue; then the piece was given several coats of varnish.

WOMAN WITH BASKET by John Smith, washed stones. Artist-craftsman John Smith works in numerous materials, most often on commissioned murals or large wall pieces. But for his own pleasure he frequently makes such delightful smaller pieces as this Woman with Basket from washed black, white, and gray stones, imported from Mexico. Figures are not easy to handle effectively, but here the great economy of the design and interesting relationship of gray, black, and white makes for simple drama. ▶

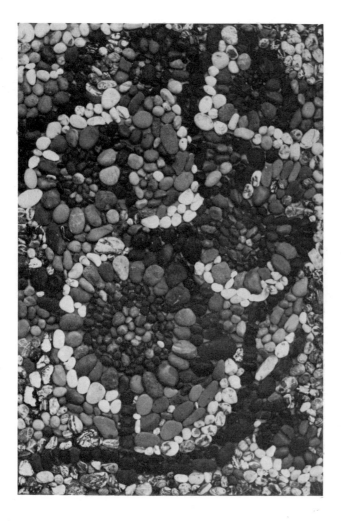

SUNFLOWERS by Betty Dike, pebbles and rocks. Betty Dike derives inspiration for her handsome pebble mosaics from frequent trips to the Big Sur country with her painter husband, Phil Dike. Along the beautiful coastline, she gathers pebbles that have remarkable variety in color.

She begins her work with a rough sketch, usually drawn on the driftwood that she prefers for a background, since it is a good natural tone for her purpose. Then she works directly with the pebbles, placing, rearranging, and shifting them about until the design is the way she likes it. All pieces are fastened to the board with a clear white glue (polyvinyl acetate).

All her ideas for designs stem from nature — among them birds, butterflies, pine trees, and flowers. Sunflowers offer the theme for this swirling panel with a design of flowers and stems that move rhythmically upward.

BUTTERFLIES by Betty Dike create a delightful pattern made of pebbles. Collection, Sue Smith, Laguna Beach, California. ▶

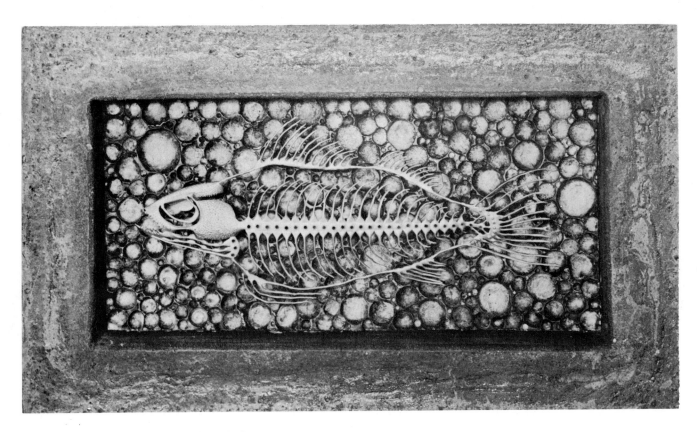

PANEL by Emile Norman. This skeleton of a fish was laid in natural stones, then set in cement.

WHITE ON WHITE by Glen Michaels, for Embassy Tour Exhibit sponsored by Mrs. Estes Kefauver, Washington, D.C. White tile, porcelain, and pottery fragments were mounted on wood (36" x 40") in a swirling abstract pattern. ▶

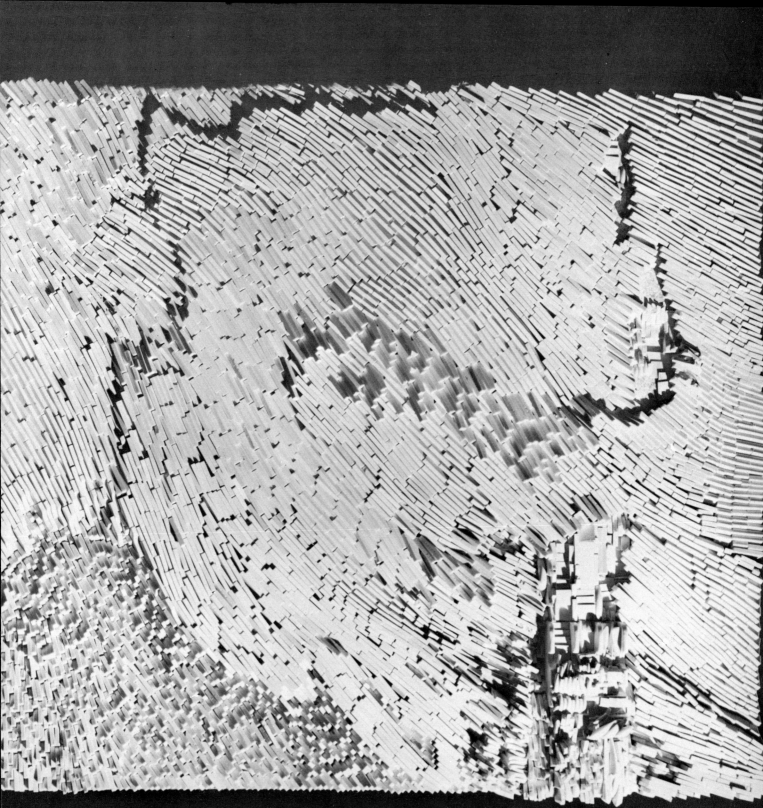

GALLERY PIECE by Glen Michaels. Black shale and wood were assembled spontaneously as the artist worked in a freehand manner. Pieces were fastened to the wood (48" diameter) base with a petroleum adhesive. Collection, Detroit Institute of Art.

GALLERY PIECE by Glen Michaels, Exhibited Triennale, Milan, Italy, 1964. The panel was made from black shale and Roman stone, mounted on wood (30" x 48") with no finish used. Collection, Mr. and Mrs. Jack Goodman, Los Angeles, California. ▶

ENDOMOSAIC by Emile Norman. This artist is credited with being the first to use natural leaves and foliage between two sheets of Plexiglas, a variation of the mosaic technique which he has named Endomosaic. He places a sheet of Plexiglas over a light table and the tesserae are glued into place with transparent adhesive. He works with a wide range of bits and pieces, including found objects — anything from stained glass to seashells. When all the materials are fastened with transparent adherent, they are then sealed in liquid plastic and the second sheet of Plexiglas is then bonded over them, forming a kind of sandwich.

6. CERAMIC MOSAIC

In the unusual medium of ceramic mosaic, we find the originality, skill and imagination usually associated with the work of F. Carlton Ball, Professor of Fine Arts at the University of Southern California.

Here the artist did not set out to achieve a specific pattern, but rather to produce one with swirling motion and rhythm. Because the design was an active one he selected a low keyed scheme; he also enjoys working with neutral tones.

He first hand formed the many small pieces from three different kinds of clay.

FORMING THE CERAMIC PIECES

Buff stoneware was used for the lightest values, which resulted in gradations of buff or biscuit colored tones. Red stoneware was used for the middle tones, shades of warm brown. Red stoneware clay mixed with Barnard clay produced the darkest tones of deep blue-gray.

As Ball worked spontaneously, the clay began to take somewhat cone-shaped or rock-like pieces and rounds of varying sizes from ½" to ¾" across. The longest rock-shaped pieces measured about 1½" in their longest dimension.

After the pieces were hand formed, the round ones were textured in many ways with the end of a teaspoon, as well as the eraser and point of a pencil.

Detail of ceramic mosaic panel by F. Carlton Ball. The interesting textures on the round pieces were made with the point and the eraser end of a pencil. Petal-like forms were laid one on top of another in certain areas to give variation in depth.

After Professor Ball completed the decoration of all of the oval forms that he wished to use in his mosaic composition, they were set aside to thoroughly air dry — about three days in a dry climate. Then they were loaded into a kiln on racks and fired to 2300°F., a stoneware temperature. For craftsmen who do not have access to such a high firing kiln, a ceramic temperature of 1600°F. is adequate. The kiln was permitted to cool for twenty-four hours and then the stoneware "tesserae" were removed.

ADHERING THE CERAMIC PIECES

Designing spontaneously as he worked, Ball found that flower forms began to develop. Some of them were built up to a low relief.

These pieces were glued separately onto a ¾" plywood panel. The pieces were pressed into regular tile-setting cement that had been colored with equal parts of red iron oxide and manganese dioxide. The cement was spread onto the board like thick frosting on a cake, using a palette knife.

The total effect is much like a piece that had been created out of natural stone and rock formations.

F. Carlton Ball creates a sunburst pattern on leather-hard clay discs with the point of a pencil.

He creates texture on individual clay pieces with the round end of a spoon. Some of the pieces, already fired, are shown in the foreground. (Step 1)

Tile setting cement, colored with iron oxide, is spread on a plywood board. A knife is used to spread the setting material. (Step 2)

Ceramic pieces are set in mosaic-like fashion into the wet tile-setting cement. Each ceramic element is an interesting design in itself. (Step 3)

Here we can see the handsome pattern emerge as various shapes, sizes, colors define the pattern.

CERAMIC MOSAIC RELIEF

Mosaic techniques and ceramics were combined in this ingeniously planned panel by artist Bonnie Jean Malcolm. A full-sized sketch was first rendered on paper. A frame, 29" wide and 69" high, was then made from 1" Marine plywood. If a piece is to be used outdoors, this is better than ordinary plywood, since it contains waterproofing ingredients. To make it sturdy, the frame was both glued and nailed together. The edges were sealed off with a coat of waterproof resin.

MAKING THE LEAF FORMS

To make the ceramic leaf forms, snowflake phylodendron were cut from the bush and dried thoroughly, then soaked in a solution of black copper oxide for a period of a week. It takes at least that long to obtain a good coating. (Green leaves do not soak up as much copper as dried leaves.) Manganese or red iron oxide may also be used for different effects. A large basting dish (borrowed from the kitchen) was used as a container for the solution. Glass and enamel are also fine, but aluminum should not be used for this purpose.

When the leaves were removed from the solution, they were copperized. They were carefully drained, but still damp when set aside. A slab of clay was rolled out to ⅝" thickness. The clay was then rolled inside the wooden plywood frame, *exactly* the same size as the box, thus allowing for a small amount of shrinkage.

The copperized leaves were then placed on top of a slab of clay and, with a sharp pointed tool, the leaf forms were cut out "the way you cut fudge," or in the same way you cut out a cookie shape around a metal form. The background clay around the clay leaves was then pulled away, leaving the clay leaves to dry. When dry, they were fired in a ceramic kiln with the copperized leaves still adhering. The copper melted into the clay, producing a handsome patina. The natural leaves burned out completely in the firing. A temperature of 1800°F. is proper for this firing. The veins of the natural leaves were imprinted in the fired clay.

COMPLETING THE DESIGN

In the meantime, blue-green china pieces (from broken pottery dishes) were hammered into smaller, usable sizes. But before they were set in place, the bottom of the frame was given a thin coat of mastic applied with a palette knife.

The still smaller pieces, necessary for filling in the background, were cut to shape with nippers. Each piece was *buttered* with mastic and set in place. After they were fastened to the board, marble dust was sprinkled over the surface to fill in the crevices.

The natural color of the wood frame was lightly brazed with a torch, leaving the natural grain, then given a coat of hard paste wax.

The effect is one of low relief in closely related tones.

CERAMIC AND MOSAIC PANEL by Bonnie Jean Malcolm. Ceramic and mosaic techniques combine in making this low relief panel in which copper-treated leaves, adhered to clay forms of identical shape, are dried so that the copper is absorbed by the clay. The clay leaves are then applied to the mosaic ground made from broken china fragments.

CERAMIC MOSAIC WALL PANEL

Tom McMillin of El Segundo, California, uses a mosaic-like treatment of ceramic clay in panels that are often incorporated into architectural designs or used as wall murals, like the stoneware design shown here.

This wall panel was made by first pressing soft clay onto a concrete surface. The theme was then developed by applying further slabs and chunks of clay and working with it in this malleable condition until a harmonious flow of design was established.

Some of the detail was painted on with engobe (colored clay) and given textures by carving into certain areas, or imprinting various objects into the clay — nails, a trowel, the artist's fingers, or whatever suited his purpose. With a pointed tool, he did the deepest in-carving for still more depth and to accentuate the rhythm of the pattern.

CUTTING AND FIRING

The next step was to cut the mural into pieces to be fired. "This was not done at random," the artist explained, "nor in a grid-like pattern. Each piece was cut into a shape that emphasized the over-all pattern."

After the cutting, the mural panel was allowed to dry thoroughly on a concrete floor before placing the ceramic pieces in the kiln. A hole was drilled through each piece. Later, a bolt was put through these holes to secure the backing.

In the first firing, the mural was heated overnight and fired the next day to 1800°F. (cone 07). (If areas are to be glazed or oxides added to the surface, this is done after the bisque firing.) The piece was then placed back in the kiln for a glaze firing (which took approximately twenty-four hours from start to finish) to 235°F. in a reduction atmosphere.

ASSEMBLING AND MOUNTING

After the glaze firing, the panel was reassembled. A word of caution is added here for anyone attempting large panels of this nature: in the case of a large mural, to avoid confusion in putting it back together properly, it is wise to number the back of each piece. "I learned the hard way," says McMillin.

The next step was to mount the panels. A ¾" piece of plywood was cut to the size of the mural. The plywood was then covered with burlap, and over that a coat of epoxy resin was spread. The stoneware pieces were arranged on the resin and bolted to the plywood for additional security. The mural panel was then ready for installation.

This may be done in many ways. Small panels are hung on the wall like a picture. Large ones (such as the mural illustrated here) are bolted to and *through* the wall, and fastened to the studding.

The approximate weight of this mural panel is ten pounds to the square foot. The size of the individual panels is 2' x 10'.

CERAMIC MOSAIC MURAL by Tom McMillin, ceramic (stoneware) mural made in a mosaic-like technique. McMillin often works with architects to create special pieces, such as this one, for both private residences and public buildings. This piece is installed in the main entrance to the Design Center Building in Los Angeles, California. Individual panels are 2' x 10'.

7. WOOD MOSAICS

Wood has very special qualities, not the least of them being its subtle colorations. They range from golds (such as those found in golden oak) to the rich browns of mahogany and walnut to the more exotic vermilion, purple heart, and rare ebony woods. Wood is also pleasant to handle and modern craftsmen are finding new ways to utilize it in mosaic and mosaic-like techniques.

Wood may be purchased at a lumber yard; the widest selection will be found in a lumber yard that handles hardwoods. It may also be found on beaches, usually fragmented; in the woods, of course; even in the desert. We have already discussed the use of discarded wooden scraps in the chapter on found objects, so this chapter will relate more specifically to the formal use of wood.

It is understandable that sculptors who enjoy working in wood might find it challenging to experiment with mosaic techniques as an extension of their own skills. Depending on the choice and combinations of the materials and the finish — waxed, rubbed satin-smooth, stained, or merely given several coats of clear varnish — the effect can be primitive in feeling, sophisticated, or purely decorative.

On the following pages, we show the work of three talented artists. Two of them are sculptors; one was formerly a painter. Their techniques vary greatly. Their finished works are dissimilar, but

PANEL by Glen Michaels. Wood scraps, mounted on a 38" x 40" wood panel, are left with a natural finish. Private collection.

each one uses wood as his material; each has created an art form uniquely his own which may inspire your own creativity.

WOOD MOSAIC RELIEFS

Charles Schlein is a serious sculptor who works in many materials, but primarily in wood. Being an experimenter, he has pioneered the wood mosaic surface. Often utilizing scraps chiseled away from larger figures, he cuts each mosaic piece to the desired shape and size. Then he cements, grouts, or dowels them into a wooden base or panel. Birds, heads of women, and clowns are among his preferred subjects.

Vermilion wood, purple heart, silver hare wood from England, pink eucalyptus from California, orange wood, osage are a few of the many unusual varieties used for color and texture in his wood mosaic designs.

In *Harlequin*, Schlein has used a low relief technique in a narrow, horizontal panel, completely set in small wooden pieces. Orange and vermilion were among the woods of many colors he used, in keeping with the lively theme of his design. The wood was polished with wax and a soft rag to bring out the grain and accentuate its gentle beauty.

HARLEQUIN by Charles Schlein, full length panel in wood relief, overlaid with wood mosaic. The design was drawn directly onto the wooden panel on which the mosaic was then laid. Wooden tiles are set in many different directions to obtain a feeling of light and movement.

Large detail of Harlequin *wood relief panel, utilizing mosaic treatment. Warm colors predominate.*

WOOD CARVING AND WOOD MOSAIC

This striking and unusual panel, *Phases of the Eclipse*, designed and executed by sculptor Robert Ortlieb, combines many textures and the use of many types of wood.

Since the panel was to represent a symbolic idea, it was first worked out in an abstract design. Three ink sketches were made to obtain a feeling of the movement and to indicate the general course and flow of the motion.

From these ink sketches, a three-dimensional sketch in terracotta was evolved as a further development of the theme.

PLANNING THE DESIGN

On a piece of plywood, the general rhythm of the design was marked off — a rough sketch that served as a tentative guide. This was done in white chalk so that it might be easily erased.

Abstract shapes of each symbol were then cut out of heavy paper. The cloud-like form representing the sun's corona was also cut from this same cardboard.

The artist began with a full circle. (In full eclipse, all you see is the edge of the sun coming around; this is symbolic of the full eclipse.) These cardboard abstract shapes were juggled about on the sheet of plywood, shifting until the design was completely satisfactory to the artist in its rhythmic pattern of shapes. Then the work began on the separate wood pieces of the mosaic.

CARVING THE WOOD PIECES

The various textures, colors, and types of wood produced a rich range of coloration throughout the design, including vermilion wood (a deep vermilion shade); purple heart, with its handsome lavender tones; genereco for the warm browns; lignum vitae; heart wood and sap wood (a greenish black to yellow); flowering acacia; redwood burl; ebony; and pepper tree wood.

The variety of wood shapes contributed to the interest, but also demanded careful designing and skillful planning in assembling so many separate pieces and still retaining an over-all sense of unity. For this reason, the entire design made up from the cut paper shapes (the ones that would eventually be made in *wood*) was taped onto the board in order to study the relationships of the forms until a perfectly pleasing design was apparent.

The carvings were done by hand with an electric sander, electric drill, several types of scoop chisels, and rifflers to go around corners and scoop out wood.

COMPLETING THE PANEL

After the individual pieces were carved, they were carefully sanded with fine garnet paper — more durable than sandpaper. Since epoxy resin has a tendency to darken the wood, a clear plastic glue was used for the setting, done on a ¾" mahogany plywood base panel. Long-pronged tweezers helped separate the small pieces of wood tesserae cut to size. The carved pieces were fastened with screws through the back of the panel.

The border which frames the panel was made from English walnut.

Because of the sharp corners on some of the carved pieces, a soft rag was not practical for wiping on the final coating of wax, although a rag may be used to polish the flat areas. Here, a brush was used to spread a good quality commercial furniture wax over the piece, and into the fine crevices and corners. A toothbrush and small scrub brush were used to polish the wood to a satin sheen that brought out the true beauty of the multi-colored grains of the many handsome pieces of inlaid wood.

Preliminary sketch made with a stick of wood dipped in ink for a relief mosaic panel, Phases of the Eclipse, by Robert Ortlieb. The sketch is an abstraction made to show the general rhythm of the design and the tentative placement of various wood pieces.

Another development of the eclipse theme, this time three-dimensional, in terracotta, which gives a truer picture of what the final result will be. The final panel will be in both low and high relief, with intricate carvings and insets.

Some of the pieces shown in the sketches begin to take shape in wood. The picture also shows some of the pieces cut out of thin white cardboard and put in place on the panel. These will all eventually be cut out of wood. Being lightweight, they can be easily shifted about on the panel until the final placement is determined.

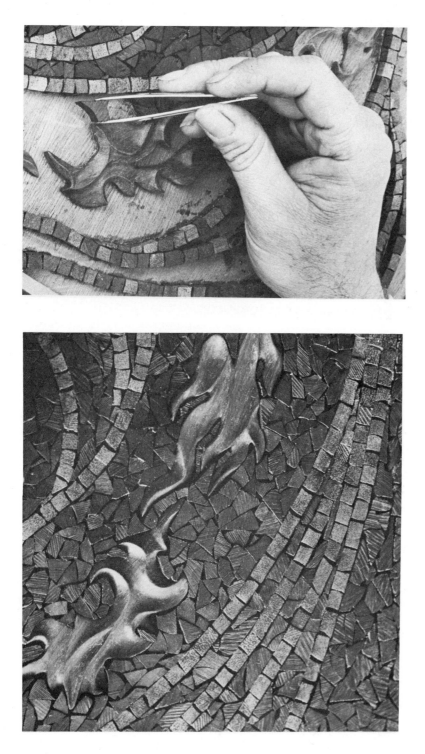

Here the artist uses a long-pronged tweezers to place a piece of ebony against a leaf-like scroll of purple heart wood.

Detail showing carving and inlay pattern of wooden "tiles" set into place on the panel.

PHASES OF THE ECLIPSE by Robert Ortlieb. Here is the finished panel, the result of excellent craftsmanship, imagination, and a refined sense of color and design. Notice how the carefully planned carvings create a feeling of continuous movement. The panel was finished off with a narrow band of wood to set off and unify the intricate design. ▶

WOOD CONSTRUCTIONS

The work that Mabel Hutchinson does today in wood was first inspired by the small pieces of wood that fall to the floor of the woodworking shop which she and her husband operate in Capistrano Beach, California. These fragments are free forms in interesting shapes, as well as the usual round, rectangular, and square forms. They are the finest hardwood, both domestic and imported. Today, her time is completely taken up with the making of wooden doors with mosaic-like decorative surface treatment, architectural panels, totems, and sculpture.

Wood, glue, stains, and color are the chief ingredients of her work. The pieces combine the use of softwoods, teak, mahogany, maple, birch, oak, and such exotic imports as zebra wood from Africa and East Indian rosewood, among others.

Here is her own account of how she works: "To create a small panel from my wood pieces, I begin with a panel of exterior plywood. I then spread out my boxes of accumulated pieces, selecting and eliminating, sorting and planning.

"I begin by placing my choicest pieces upon the blank plywood. I start with no set design in mind, but I have a procedure that I adhere to strictly. My plan is to create order out of chaos without doing the obvious. I try at all times to avoid the ordinary. I delight in creating surprises, to stimulate interest in the pieces. I sometimes work for a week just shifting loose pieces about on the sheet of plywood until I think I have just the effect I want. Then I begin to use sandpaper and glue. I use no stains or color until the piece is finished."

DOORS by Mabel Hutchinson, 8' x 6'. Many free-form shapes combine with discs and rectangles in this handsome pair of double doors in which every piece is screwed in place from the back. The panels can be screwed to existing doors.

DOORS by Mabel Hutchinson, wood construction. Many shapes of imported and domestic hardwood pieces are combined in this unusual pair of 6' x 6' 8" doors which were first displayed at the Pasadena Art Museum All California Design Show in 1965.

▶

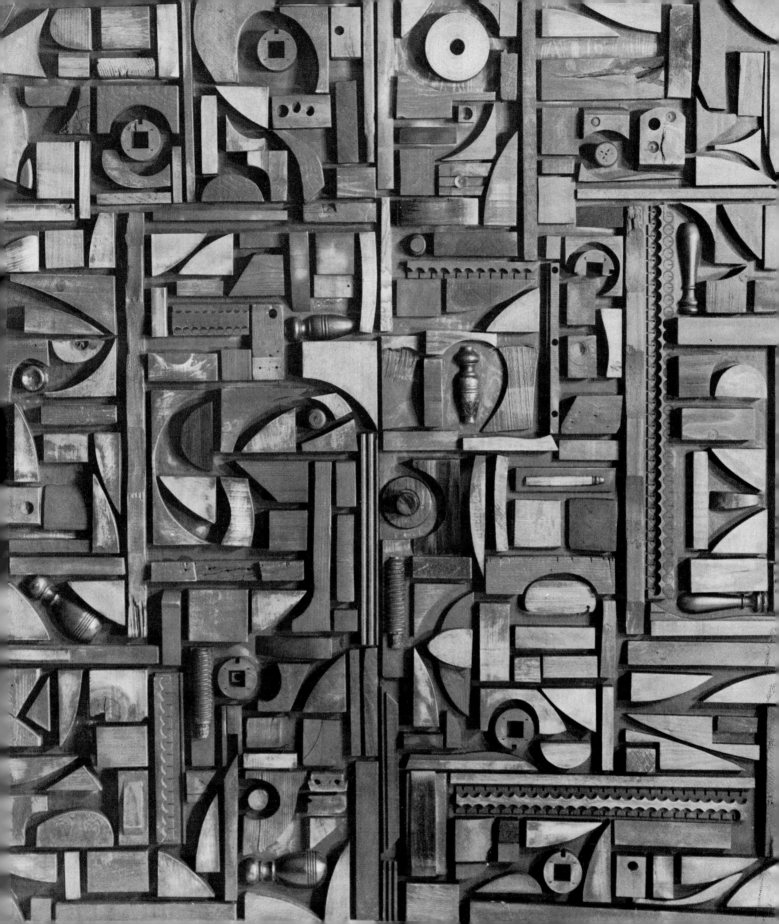

8. NAIL MOSAICS

CONFIGURATION by David Partridge, nail mural and divider, 8' x 8'. This nail mural also serves as a divider in the Shanklin Hotel on the Isle of Wight.

In 1958, British artist David Partridge began working with ordinary nails as an extension of the abstract forms he was then painting. With these commonplace materials, he has managed to produce an extraordinary art form, uniquely his own, although many other mosaicists are now working with nails.

Dissatisfied with the role of abstract painter, David Partridge followed an urge to make something out of the nails and small bits of lumber left over from remodeling his home. "I enjoyed the first one and went on and did a lot more." From that unpretentious beginning he has parlayed a unique talent into a rewarding career and an international reputation. His work has found its way into the permanent collections of the Tate Gallery, London; the Museum of Contemporary Art, Santiago, Chile; the Library of Congress, Washington, D.C., among many others. His commissioned work includes pieces executed for public buildings in many countries of the world.

Materials required for his work are few and easily available: hammer, nails, ¾" to 1" plywood or other heavy board. Paint, burlap, or another fabric is sometimes used to cover the board if the design suggests it. His nail mosaics range in size from 12" wall panels to 32' murals.

117

TYPES OF NAILS

All types of nails have possibilities — anything from a thin panel nail with a thickened end to a 3″ springhead nail with a ½″ wide head. To date, Partridge has experimented with better than two dozen varieties, but he is always looking for new ones. However, he prefers to use no more than *three* types on a single piece.

"I use largely galvanized nails, subsequently lacquered to avoid rust and also to give a somewhat glazed quality to the nailheads." The nails are driven in straight, the longer ones about ½″ into the wood surface. An occasional slip of the hand may turn out to be a happy accident and the crooked nails then turn into an interesting design treatment.

Partridge's early work was quite spontaneous and grew more or less automatically after he had hammered the first nail. "Later I developed a vocabulary of what happens with different nails and the treatment of them."

When a work is commissioned, the artist must obviously furnish the client with some sort of sketch or design. Partridge keeps these very small in order to have as much freedom as possible; this allows a great deal of what he calls "intuitive creation" in the final work. Otherwise, if no preliminary sketch is required, he starts by making a few light marks on the surface to be covered and from there on builds spontaneously.

TEXTURES

All manner of textures may be explored in working with nails. Simple or intricate, smooth or bas-relief surfaces can be achieved. Motifs may be abstract or formalized patterns. Some of Partridge's most effective designs have been executed in low relief. Others have cratered surfaces. Some of the extremely decorative pieces are small; very thin nails of varying lengths are combined and closely set to create patterns which have the appearance of fine lace or needlework.

"Obviously the technique, nails with polished heads of varying lengths, and the like, could well be applied to figurative designs," he points out. "But as far as I'm concerned at the moment, the idea of the created 'thing' is of utmost importance. To draw a figure and fill it with nails would simply reduce the whole thing to a craft and the subsequent hammering would be drudgery! The unexpected still crops up and is the most satisfying."

CORAL CONFIGURATION by David Partridge, nail mosaic, 4' x 8'. In this configuration, the lacy texture of coral is emulated by the use of fine nails in free form "stripes" and small circle patterns against a background of tacks with round pin heads. Executed for the Coral Beach Hotel in Beirut, Lebanon. ▶

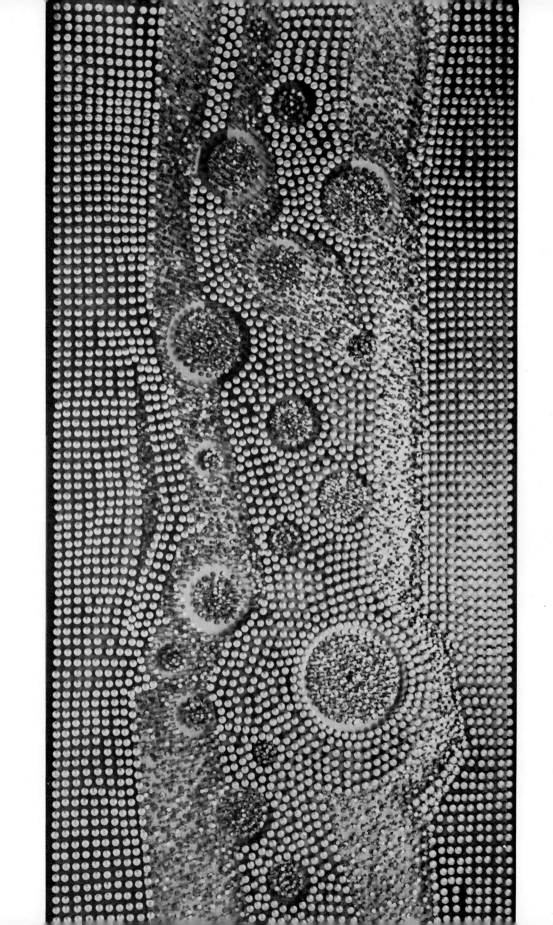

CRATERED CONFIGURATION by
David Partridge, nail mosaic, 3' x 6'.
A nail panel with a design of unusual
distinction. Notice how the nails are
placed sideways in the larger motif
(left) giving star-like points to the
circular design in low relief.

120

COLUMN by David Partridge, nail mosaic. This totemesque column stands 8' high. Although it is done entirely with nails, its appearance has somewhat the quality of old embroidery. Notice how the small nails are driven into the side of the column, giving the fringed look of fabric. ▶

MOONSCAPE by David Partridge, nail mosaic, detail of a ceiling. The background was first painted coppery gold and silver before the plain copper nails, springhead nails, and galvanized clouts with polished heads were hammered into it. Copper gleaming against copper, polished nail heads against silver, all create a richly glowing surface that changes with each change of light. Nails set in circles give a cratered appearance. Detail of ceiling for Royal Roof Restaurant, Royal Garden, Kensington. Made for Design Research Unit, London.

9. MOSAIC SCULPTURE

THE DIN OF YOUTH by Patricia Burg, mosaic relief panel. Patricia Burg began The Din of Youth *by making a small sketch showing the negative shapes. A plywood panel was then coated with magnesite. The relief was built up with plaster, the forms cut out and shaped with small knives and spatulas. While the plaster was wet, the phrase, "These games and this clatter of arms is the din of youth." was cut into it. Epoxy resin was used to set the tesserae, which are placed at various angles to create texture.*

Sculpture has undergone many changes during the past few decades and modern sculptors are constantly reaching for new ways to express form. Constructions of wood built as a child builds with blocks, kinetic sculptures, ceramic forms, and welded metal figures have called forth their inventiveness.

Many modern craftsmen have found interesting ways of incorporating mosaic into their sculptured pieces. Bonnie Jean Malcolm's fascination for the primitive figures of ancient civilizations — figures whose surfaces were covered with bits of vitreous materials — led her to make some unusual pieces of her own. In her *Primitive Duck* with its strange foreshortening, we find the influence of early Mexican artisans.

MODELING THE BASIC FORM

Here the form was made out of terracotta, then fired to cone 03 to produce an extremely hard body surface.

With black leather dye, areas of black were painted on either side of the form for the sole purpose of defining the planes. With a palette knife, black mastic was spread over the area to be embedded with tesserae, a small area at one time. This was continued until the entire piece was completed.

125

SETTING THE TESSERAE

Venetian tesserae were used in shades of blue and white. The 1″ glass tesserae were cut to the shapes and sizes needed.

To simulate feathers, some of the glass pieces were shaped to oblongs and set at an angle. This helps create a feeling of rhythm and adds interest and depth to the over-all texture.

Darker tiles were used to outline the eyes and a darker bead was used for the eyes themselves. The figure was then grouted. A small amount of color was added to the grout to give it a soft, neutral tone.

The primitive form of the duck was modeled in terracotta, then fired to cone 03. The planes of the form are indicated with black leather dye brushed onto either side of the piece. A palette knife smears on the black mastic into which the tesserae are to be set.

The artist begins to set tesserae into the black mastic.

With a palette knife, black mastic is smeared over a small section at a time. Then tesserae are set into that area.

Detail of tesserae set at an angle. This helps to give the appearance of feathers following the contour of the bird, and adds interesting texture to the surface.

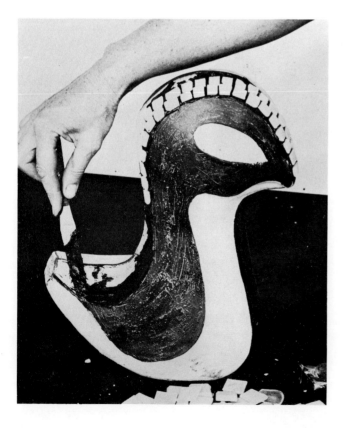

INLAY

The craft of inlay dates back to early beginnings in Venetian work of the 14th Century, primarily in wood inlaid on wooden boxes. Among the handsomest combinations were ivory inlaid upon black wood or walnut wood. Various other types of materials have been used in making inlays: metal, tortoise shell, ivory, even precious stones. But wood has always been a favorite material for use in inlay and most of us are familiar with wood in this technique.

Many of the early inlays were produced by first making a sketch on paper, pasting the wooden pieces to the paper on which the design was made, then proceeding very much in the manner in which mosaics are made today by the *reverse* or *indirect* method (see Chapter 2).

Few contemporary craftsmen have the patience, the time, or the great skill demanded of so exacting and intricate a technique. Sometimes simpler pieces are made by isolated craftsmen in various sections of the country. Emile Norman, however, has gained an international reputation for his work in this demanding technique.

As in all the other mediums in which he works, Norman approaches this one in a personal and very original way. Since the medium is so complex and dependent on excellence of craftsmanship, it is not for the novice. But we show it here as an example of what the truly creative mind can conceive and, hopefully, to inspire other craftsmen to work in a personalized pioneering manner, developing their own mosaic sculpture techniques.

The following is a brief resume of the way Emile Norman (with the aid of his working partner, Brooks Clement) goes about making three dimensional inlaid pieces.

MODELING WAX FORM

The three-dimensional forms of fish, bird, or

PRIMITIVE DUCK by Bonnie Jean Malcolm, mosaic over terracotta. Here is the completed bird form. Shades of blue range from delicate to deep tones, combined with white. Beads are used for the eyes. Grouting gives a unifying, finishing touch to the work.

animal are first modeled from a wax-like substance of Norman's own invention. The wax-like substance, which is similar to clay, may be heated and reheated.

COMPLETING THE INLAY

Small wooden pieces of various sizes, shapes, and types of wood are then inlaid over the surface of the form. The effect is usually one of subtle coloration in closely related tones. For contrast, woods such as ebony and English hare wood (a light silvery tone) are combined, to mention just one example.

The epoxy resins are combined with pulverized woods, or sawdust, to bind the pieces together. When the mosaic design is finished, the result is a wooden sculpture with an inlaid pattern on the outside — a shell of wood-epoxy and inlaid pieces — and the wax-like substance on the inside. The wood is cured over a very low electric heat, while the wax-like substance liquefies, to be removed from the form later, thus leaving it *hollow on the inside.*

SCALE MODELS FOR PRESENTATION

Scale models are made for presentation to clients before the finished piece is executed. They are models in meticulous workmanship. Norman strives to emulate, as closely as possible, the actual materials to be used on the finished job, whether it be cement, plastic, wood, silver, glass, or clay. No detail is too trivial to be ignored.

It is this kind of attention given to detail in every phase of his work that is partially responsible for Norman's achievement in the difficult medium of inlay.

TULE BIRD by Emile Norman, inlay sculpture, 20" long. Notice the exquisite detail of the ebony, benin, ivory, and holly wood used in the decorative surface of this figure.

FINCH by Emile Norman, inlay sculpture. Unexpected accents of white and black add charm to this design. Collection, R. Morrisey and K. Bington.

DOVE by Emile Norman, inlay sculpture. Collection Mr. and Mrs. Arthur Dahl, Pebble Beach, California.

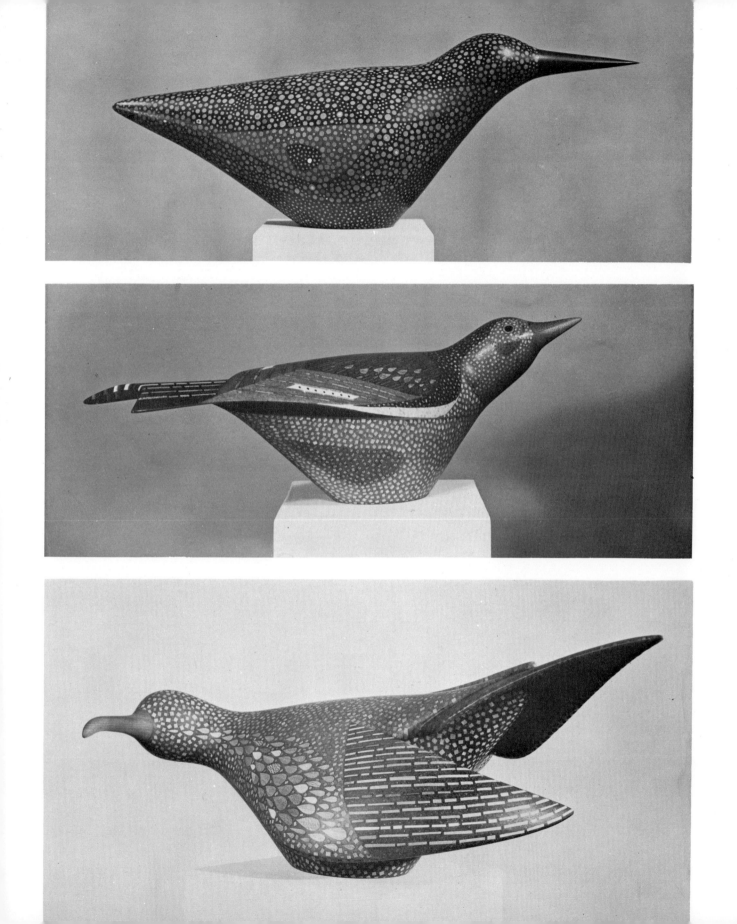

GUINEA FOWL by Emile Norman, inlay sculpture. The black of ebony and the white of ivory are the only two materials used in this stunning inlay. Collection, Mr. & Mrs. Grover M. Herman, Pebble Beach, California.

CALICO CAT by Emile Norman, inlay sculpture, 23" long. Many types of wood and the highly stylized design of the inlay make this sculpture of wood inlay particularly delightful. Collection, Cummins Catherwood.

◄

FOUR FACES OF WOMAN by Charles Schlein, wood mosaic sculpture. The artist began by carving the form of a woman's head. Small pieces of wood of various types and colors were cut to size. Each piece was glued in place separately, with special attention given to the placement of color and its relationship to the development of the features. On each of the four sides, a different face appears. Lignum vitae, vermilion wood, and walnut were a few of the woods used in this three-dimensional form. It was given added height and importance by building it up on a wooden base. With a soft rag, the sculpture was polished until a satin sheen was achieved.

10. MOSAIC TECHNIQUES FOR SCHOOLS

In the foregoing chapters, you have been exposed to various materials and their possibilities. You have seen how artists have transformed the most unlikely materials into pieces that are unique, beautiful, even humorous. You have observed the ways in which artists with imagination have utilized things as different in texture and form as rusty nails and luxurious hard woods. In each instance, these elements have been used to accommodate a personal sense of design.

Once you are even slightly aware of the potential of materials, you will find yourself searching out new ones. Teachers are constantly on the lookout for ideas to use in arts and crafts classes — often with a rather limited budget in mind. In this chapter, you will see the work of teachers, and students whose ages range from nine to fourteen years; the efforts of individual students and joint ventures in which as many as thirty-five students have participated. There are also several pieces by persons working in other creative fields, from which they occasionally depart to do something that satisfies a particular creative urge — or just for the fun of doing it!

In the following pages we deal with mosaics made from things found around the house — materials that are particularly suitable for classroom use. Let's start in the kitchen!

Melissa Penny thoughtfully selects the dried foods to be used in a mosaic.

MOSAICS FROM THE KITCHEN

In this room, rich with materials, consider the potential of dried beans, peas, lentils, pumpkin seeds, sunflower seeds, rice, bird seed, and the numerous members of the pasta family. Pasta cartwheels, with their open lattice work, seashells, noodles with crimped edges, even elbow macaroni and spaghetti have aesthetic qualities when used with imagination.

These kitchen "found materials" are varied in shape and size and have subtle colorings. They can be painted with any water base paint, from poster color to acrylic. They may be mixed or matched, making sure, however, that there is sufficient contrast in sizes and color to bring out a design effectively.

The materials can be mounted on plywood or heavy cardboard, or worked out on styrofoam. The latter is good because it is flexible, lightweight, easy to handle. It can be bought in preformed shapes of which stars, trees, and wreaths are only a few. But it can also be purchased in a solid piece, then cut or whittled to a size and shape you want.

Unless you are experienced in crafts and can work spontaneously in design, it is a good idea to make a sketch beforehand of what you have in mind. It may be only a suggestion, but at least it will guide you in the way you want to go.

In any event, it is the *light touch* that will determine your success in working with these materials. Keep your designs simple and well defined. Do not use too many shapes in one piece of work. Avoid fussiness.

EGGSHELL MOSAICS

A very old and beautiful material for use in mosaic is the eggshell. To prepare eggshells for use as mosaic tesserae, punch a hole in each end of the egg and blow the contents out. (A very large omelette is usually a fringe benefit of eggshell mosaics.) When enough eggs have been emptied to provide what is estimated to be enough shells to cover the panel, each eggshell should be painted a solid color. Watercolor, casein, acrylic paints, or even food dye may be used. Leave some eggs uncolored to provide the white areas that may be needed in the composition.

After you have a range of colors that you feel is sufficient, break the shells into small pieces about the size of a fingernail. Try to get as many square and rectangular pieces as possible. Then draw your design on a rigid board, anything from cardboard to plywood. Apply a coat of polyvinyl acetate glue (white glue) to a small area and set the eggshell "tesserae" into the glue. Develop the composition in this way section by section. Place the shells close together because there is no reason to grout an eggshell mosaic and it looks better if a minimum of panel area shows between the joints of the tesserae.

SOME SUGGESTIONS ABOUT COLOR

Heavy colors destroy the delicate appearance of the pasta and this delicacy is part of its charm. The pieces are ornate in themselves and need no deep or bright shadings. Off-white is generally the most effective. At times, gold is used to advantage, especially in decorations for Christmas. Or with an atomizer or brush, the pieces may be tipped with gold, silver, or pastel tones.

Dried beans, peas, lentils, and similar materials also have innately handsome, subtle colors which it is often best to leave unpainted. It may also be effective to paint *some* of these elements and experiment with the interplay of painted and unpainted materials. If the student prefers to paint them — by brushing, dipping, or spraying — it is worth remembering that too many intense colors may cancel one another.

PAPER MOSAICS

Paper is the least expensive and most easily available of all craft materials. Look for interesting papers in gift wrappings, Christmas wrappings and cards, magazine advertisements, postcards, candy box linings, among other discards. You can buy packages of kindergarten paper in a rainbow of solid colors at a minimal cost. You can even use newspaper in certain parts of your paper mosaic design.

Lightweight colored cardboard is good for cutting paper "tiles." These have a slightly raised look and you can build up a surface in this way.

Try combining paper mosaic with other techniques such as collage, applique, incising, and painted decoration.

PLANNING THE DESIGN

In any event, start by drawing your pattern first. If it is to be a spontaneous pattern, sketch in your idea very lightly with a pencil — just enough so that you can follow it without much trouble. If the design is to be formal and precise, begin by drawing it more carefully on paper. You will save yourself aggravation if you first sketch on tracing paper. Being transparent, it enables you to see what you are doing when you transfer the design. Then trace your design directly onto the cardboard background, using carbon paper between the transparent paper and the background board.

If it helps you to get the feeling of the mosaic technique, square off your tracing paper first. You may not want to trace the entire pattern onto the cardboard; this may be too restricting. Trace whatever you think may be difficult to execute *without* its being traced.

If you want your paper tile to move symmetrically throughout the design, you will, of course, have to be exact. If the tiles, themselves, are to be reasonably symmetrical in shape, you will have to measure them. With heavy scissors, cut layers of

tile at one time. Your own ingenuity will tell you the way you enjoy working most. Whatever you do, have *fun* doing it!

RUBBER CEMENT

Various types of paper paste are usable, but for all practical purposes, rubber cement is best. It allows you to be freer, to make changes as you go, to move things about with the least amount of mess. It allows you to experiment freely.

Making a paper mosaic has advantages other than being merely attractive. It can be helpful as a preliminary study of the one you plan to make in more permanent materials. You can avoid making mistakes by making a mosaic first in paper — rather than in tesserae. The paper mosaic will give you a fair idea of how your design will look when it is finally executed in more expensive tesserae materials, which are less easily altered.

Illustrated in this chapter are paper mosaics of varied types. Some incorporate other techniques with the paper tiles. Some are spontaneous patterns; others are quite formalized. Most of the examples were made by elementary school children.

PAPER MOSAICS BY CHILDREN

Children have a directness that is refreshing and teachers will find this dramatically displayed in paper mosaics.

In the work shown on the following pages, notice how the children have, in each instance, concentrated on one simple motif which gives the design an immediate center of interest. Although the backgrounds are made from many separate strips and pieces of cut paper, these never overpower the main subjects of birds, fish, trees, fruit, butterflies, stars, etc.

With great inventiveness, advertisements from magazines were cut into small rectangular, square and diamond shapes. Bits of wrapping paper and thin colored cardboard were also used. After these paper pieces were arranged in a design that satisfied the artist, they were fastened onto the paper background with vegetable glue, rubber cement, or other types of paper glue.

The paper mosaics shown here were made by fifth and sixth grade students, ranging from nine to ten years of age, at the Third Street Elementary School in Los Angeles, California. The project was assigned by fifth and sixth grade teacher, Dorothy McKee, who supervised their work. The assignment was made around the Christmas holidays. The children were told that the theme *could* suggest Christmas, but not necessarily — it was left up to them. Patterns were first drawn on paper, and it was emphasized that the design should be kept simple, devoid of meaningless detail, and that it must fill the space in which the student worked. For power and boldness of conceptions, these designs can vie with many of the professional examples in this book.

PASTA MOSAIC SCULPTURE by Helen Luitjens, head of the art department of Paul Revere Junior High School, Brentwood, California. Strips of ruffle edged noodles, straight pieces of spaghetti, elbow macaroni, cartwheels, and one row of pasta shells were used to make the cone-shaped table decoration at left. Notice how the various shapes are closely grouped in specific areas, not mixed helter-skelter all over the form. The piece was sprayed a dull gold. A small Christmas ball was placed on top.

Seashells, short ends of elbow macaroni, and cartwheels create an elegant holiday wreath (center). Small pieces of pasta with ruffled edges divide the design at intervals; this creates a better design and simplifies it. The wreath was sprayed off-white.

Seashells, spiraling curls of pasta, and bow knots are combined in a winding pattern around a styrofoam cone shape (right). The piece and the base of styrofoam were sprayed off-white.

WALL PANEL by Stephanie Gruenberg, seed mosaic. Using dried beans, peas, rice, tapioca, and other materials recruited from her kitchen shelves, the artist has produced a formal design (first executed on paper) that is handsome enough to grace any living room. The natural brown and golden tones and the off-whites of the materials are given added richness with several heavy coats of clear lacquer.

Detail of seed mosaic by Stephanie Gruenberg. See how the strong design and contrasting values give character to this piece made from materials found in the kitchen. Lima beans, kidney beans, dried beans, and peas give handsome color to the piece. The materials are arranged in a rich encrustation to make them appear jewel-like.

Another detail of Stephanie Gruenberg's seed mosaic panel made from materials found in the kitchen. The design has unusual elegance because of the formal treatment and the excellent craftsmanship of the artist.

DRIED FOOD AND SEED MOSAICS BY CHILDREN. Both abstractions and the forms of recognizable objects are the themes of the delightful mosaics on the following pages, made by art students of Paul Revere Junior High School in Brentwood, California. Dried peas, beans, lentils, coffee grounds, and many types of pasta products were used. All the work was done under the supervision of art teacher, Helen Luitjens.

A student is shown glueing beans, corn, pebbles, tapioca, and rice to a plywood board. Kidney beans make the strong black outline around the pineapple motif.

STAR, student mosaic. Black-eye peas, coffee grounds, and small white beans are glued onto a plywood board to create a star theme.

FLOWER, student mosaic. Seeds, lima beans, dried peas, and kernels of dried corn are some of the ingredients that create this mosaic of a flower form.

BUTTERFLY, student mosaic. Dried beans and peas are used to make this striking butterfly mosaic, with its dramatic wings of coffee grounds. Here the design has the feeling of bead work. In each of these student mosaics, several coats of colorless shellac give the panel a more permanent finish.

SUN, student mosaic. The motif is treated with humor; the design is strong, with sharply contrasting values. Coffee grounds make the face of the sun. Dried beans, corn, and barley are some of the other food products used.

HORSES JUMPING A WALL, student mosaic. In this mosaic, a more complicated design has been brought off successfully. The mosaic has great charm and movement in figures made from dried peas and beans. Tapioca is used effectively on the one horse's mane. Square-shaped pasta products give a true feeling of tesserae in the wall.

ABSTRACTION, student mosaic. Note the simple, but effective use of abstract design in this satisfying arrangement of lima beans, elbow macaroni, coffee grounds, garbonza, and other dried beans and peas.

SUN, student mosaic. Another version of the sun design depends largely on the interesting proportions of the shapes and the waving movement in the sun's rays.

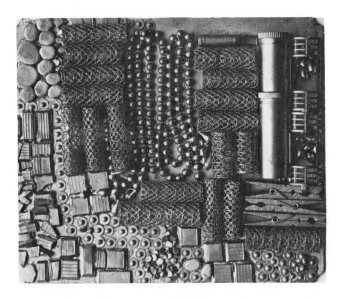

FOUND OBJECTS ASSEMBLAGE, student mosaic. Discards and some scrap wood were arranged spontaneously on plywood boards by students of Le Conte Junior High School in Los Angeles, California, under the supervision of Gerald Citrin, head of the art department. Here, pieces of broken plastic, beads, hair curlers, clothes pins, dress snaps, empty cartirdges, the handle of a razor blade, and pebbles combine to make this unusual panel that was afterwards sprayed gold.

FOUND OBJECTS ASSEMBLAGE, student mosaic. Metal chains, shells, pieces of old jewelry, hinges, twisted wire, and keys are some of the discards used in. this mosaic panel. All the objects were fastened to a plywood board with Wilhold glue, then sprayed a deep metallic gold color.

▶

BROKEN GLASS MOSAIC, student project. Bits of glass are easy to come by. Wherever you find a broken mirror, a broken soft drink bottle, or other broken glass container, you will find materials for making mosaics. Some of them have lovely colors. If the pieces are too large, place a cloth over them (for safety) and hit them gently with a lightweight hammer to obtain smaller pieces. They can also be put into a rock crusher or rolled with the side of a rolling pin. Glass bits and pieces can be embedded in grout or cement, coupled with tile or tesserae. They can also take on a new dimension when arranged on a glass panel and glued on separately. But remember that it is glass you are working with. Don't pick up fragments or brush them aside with your hands. Clear away glass bits and pieces with a soft rag or brush. This and the next panel were made by students of Paul Revere Junior High School in Brentwood, California, under the supervision of art teacher, Helen Luitjens.

BROKEN GLASS MOSAIC, student project. It is the charming arrangement of the glass "flowers" that gives this panel a special appeal. Pieces of colored glass of all sizes and shapes (all small) were arranged loosely on top of an inexpensive glass panel. Notice how the darker pieces of glass were placed to form a rhythmic pattern of their own. Each piece was glued separately onto the glass panel with Permanex. Put another piece of glass over this panel and you will have an unusual top for a coffee table. Or hang it on the wall in any dark corner that needs a bit of sparkle.

DOUBLE STAR, student mosaic. This dramatic star design combines small pebbles, tesserae, and glass fragments. Note the fine outline of pieces of tesserae around the points of the star forms; this is important here, for otherwise the design itself would be lost. Made by an eighth grade student at the Third Street Elementary School, Los Angeles. Dorothy McKee was the teacher.

JUNK MURAL, class project made by students of the Freis Avenue School, Wilmington, California, under the supervision of teacher, Dawn Pumphrey. In planning this junk mural, third grade students of the Freis Avenue School were first asked to make designs on paper for the subject, Life on an Imaginary Planet. This was a subject which they, themselves, chose. A jury of students was asked to choose various designs from which segments would be used in the final over-all pattern. Many students did no part of the actual design, but did the actual work, each putting in about seven hours' time. The entire mural was done in one month from design to completion. All students were asked to contribute materials, which included nuts, bolts, rice, dried peas and beans, pieces of roofing paper, small pebbles, even sections of broken records which, incidentally, formed the interesting texture of the sky. The panel, when completed, was given to the teacher, and now hangs in her living room.

150

Detail from Life on an Imaginary Planet, *mural made of junk and fragments by thirty-five members of the third grade class, Fries Avenue School, Wilmington, California.*

PAPER MOSAIC by Helen Luitjens. Lightweight cardboard, crayon, and incising are combined in this panel. Cardboard "tiles" were cut into many shapes and sizes. Bird and leaf forms were sketched in a freehand manner with colored wax crayons. Details of feathers and features were cut into the crayon drawings with the sharp end of a paint brush (any sharp instrument would be suitable). Colorless shellac was sprayed over the panel when finished. Tile was fastened to the cardboard with Permanex. Helen Luitjens is head of the art department, Paul Revere School, Brentwood, California.

ANGELS WITH BOUQUETS by Janice Lovoos combines paper tiles, free form paper pieces, collage. The design was first drawn on tissue paper, then traced onto the board. Light lines were drawn across the paper to indicate where the tiles would go. Chinese rice paper, Christmas wrapping paper, Christmas cards cut into tile shapes (regardless of their pattern), and solid colors cut from gift wrappings were all utilized. The angels' wings were made from the tufted lining of a candy box. Pasting was done with rubber cement.

Detail of same paper "molage," Angels with Bouquets.   ▶

Oblivious to anyone, a young mosaicist works on a paper mosaic. She first draws the design lightly on slick cardboard, then indents part of it with the point of a scissors.

Next, pieces are traced from the tissue paper design onto fancy wrapping papers used for mosaic. Here, pieces are being put into place with fingers and paper paste.

EAGLE, student mosaic in paper. The sharp contrast of dark and light values and the simple, bold form of the eagle make this paper mosaic striking. This and the next six paper mosaics were done by children in the Third Street Elementary School, Los Angeles, under the supervision of teacher, Dorothy McKee. The average age of the children was nine to ten.

BUTTERFLY, student mosaic in paper.
Accents of black on the wings and
body of the butterfly are repeated in
the background, which is made of
multi-colored strips that give movement to this mosaic pattern.

BOWL OF FRUIT, student mosaic in
paper. The vari-colored strips of the
background, contrasted with the
simple forms of the fruit and bowl,
make this a strong design.

STAR, student mosaic in paper. The small black shapes, scattered over the light ground, give balance to the star design and make it more interesting.

TREE, student mosaic in paper. A tree, made from many small pieces of paper cut from magazine ads, dominates a small panel with a background of larger rectangles.

◄

BIRD, student mosaïc in paper. The prominent accents of white on the dark feathers of the bird help to make this design rhythmic. There is also rhythm in the arrangement of the larger, free form and rectangular pieces of the background.

160

UNDERSEA SCENE, student mosaic
in paper by Donna Jean Brown, aged
twelve. The young artist chose a fish
for the main interest of her undersea pattern — made with paper cut
from advertisements — then related it
nicely to other forms of undersea life
in varied sizes and shapes. The delicate detail of the sea fern adds
charm, and the wide, black outline
unifies the entire pattern.

BIBLIOGRAPHY

Aller, Doris and Diane, *Mosaics*, (Sunset Craft Books), Lane, Menlo Park, 1959.

Anthony, E. W., *A History of Mosaics*, Porter Sargent, Boston, 1935.

Argiro, Larry, *Mosaic Art Today*, International Textbook, Scranton, 1961.

Arvois, Edmund, *Making Mosaics*, Sterling, New York, 1964.

Bitterman, Eleanor, *Art in Modern Architecture*, Reinhold, New York, 1952.

Bovini, Giuseppe, *Ravenna Mosaics*, New York Graphic Society, Greenwich, 1956.

Carls, E. W., and Wines, L. S., *The Art of Tile Setting*, Charles Bennett, Peoria, 1954.

Cennini, Cennino, *The Craftsman's Handbook*, translated by D. V. Thompson, Dover, New York, 1959.

Cetto, Anna Maria, *The Ravenna Mosaics*, Taplinger, New York, 1960.

Damaz, Paul, *Art in European Architecture*, Reinhold, New York, 1956.

Diamond, Freda, *The Story of Glass*, Harcourt, Brace and World, New York, 1953.

Forlati, Ferdinando, and Toesca, P., *Mosaics of St. Marks*, New York Graphic Society, Greenwich, 1958.

Brabar, Andre, and Chatzidakis, Manolis, *Greece, Byzantine Mosaics*, New York Graphic Society, Greenwich, 1960.

Grabar, Andre, *Byzantine Painting*, (Skira), World, New York, 1953.

Graf, Don, *Thin-Setting Bed Methods and Materials*, Tile Council of America, New York, 1952.

Graf, Don, *Tile Handbook*, Tile Council of America, New York, 1951.

Hendrickson, Edwin, *Mosaics: Hobby and Art*, Hill and Wang, New York, 1957.

Herberts, Kurt, *Complete Book of Artists' Techniques*, Praeger, New York, 1958.

Janeway, Carol, *Ceramics and Pottery Making for Everyone*, Tudor, New York, 1950.

Jenkins, Louisa, and Mills, Barbara, *The Art of Making Mosaics*, Van Nostrand, Princeton, 1957.

Journal of Glass Studies, Vols. I, II, III, and IV, Corning Museum of Glass, Corning, 1962.

Maiuri, Amadeo, *Roman Painting*, (Skira), World, New York, 1953.

Mary Magdalen, Sister, *Mosaics for Everyone*, Helen Lee, Los Angeles, 1958.

Neuberg, Frederic, *Ancient Glass*, translated by Michael Bullock and Alisa Jaffe, University of Toronto, Toronto, 1962.

Neumayer, Heinrich, *Byzantine Mosaics*, Crown, New York, 1964.

Powers, Harry Huntington, *Mosaics*, University Prints, Newton, 1938.

Prince, David Talbot, *Mosaics: The Beginnings of Christian Art*, Hodder, London, 1957.

Reynal, Jeanne, *Mosaics of Jeanne Reynal*, edited by Dore Ashton, Wittenborn, 1963.

Schapiro, Meyer, and Michael Avi-Yonah, *Israel, Ancient Mosaics*, New York Graphic Society, Greenwich, 1960.

Solon, Leon V., *Polychromy*, Architectural Record, New York, 1924.

Stieri, Emanuele, *Concrete and Masonry*, Barnes & Noble, New York, 1956.

Striblings, Mary L., *Mosaic Techniques: New Aspects of Fragmented Design*, Crown, New York, 1965.

Sweeney, J. J., and Sert, J. L., *Antonio Gaudi*, Praeger, New York, 1960.

Turquoise Mosaic Art in Ancient Mexico, Museum of the American Indian, Heye Foundation, New York, 1922.

Unger, Hans, *Practical Mosaics*, (Studio), Viking, New York, 1965.

Vasari, Giorgio, *Vasari on Technique*, edited by G. Baldwin Brown, translated by Louisa S. Maclehose, Dover, New York, 1961.

The Watts Towers, edited by Kate Steinitz, Committee for Simon Rodea's Towers in Watts, Los Angeles, 1961.

Williamson, Robert, *Mosaics: Design, Construction and Assembly*, Hearthside, New York, 1963.

Young, Joseph L., *Course in Making Mosaics*, Reinhold, New York, 1961.

Young, Joseph L., *Mosaics: Principles and Practice*, Reinhold, New York, 1963.

LIST OF SUPPLIERS

Consult your local classified directory under the heading, *Mosaics*, or write directly to the manufacturers listed below for the address of the retail store nearest you which stocks that particular material.

GENERAL MOSAIC SUPPLIES:

Avalon Mfg. Corp., 128 Middleton, St., Brooklyn, New York

Bergen Arts & Crafts, Inc., Shetland Industrial Park, Box #689, Salem, Massachusetts

Economy Handicrafts, Inc., 47-11 Francis Lewis Blvd., Flushing, New York

Immerman's Crafts, Inc., 16912 Miles Ave., Cleveland, Ohio

Korsin, Inc., 1500 Cortland, Chicago, Illinois

Latco Products, 3371 Glendale Blvd., Los Angeles, California

Magnus Craft Materials, Inc., 108 Franklin St., New York, New York 10013

Stewart Clay Co., 133 Mulberry St., New York, New York

Tepping Studio Supply Co., 3517 Riverside Drive, Dayton, Ohio

SMALTI

Latco Products, 3371 Glendale Blvd., Los Angeles, California

Leo Popper & Sons, 143 Franklin St., New York, New York

Smalti may be ordered directly from Italy from:
Angelo Orsini, Venezia (418), S. Giobbe 1045
Melloni & Moretti, Murano, Fond, Cavour 17
Ugo Dona & Figlio, Murano, Venezia, Italia

BOXES FOR STORING SMALTI & MOSAICS:

Consult your local classified telephone directory under the heading, *Boxes, Cardboard.*

CERAMIC CLAYS, KILNS, AND MATERIALS

Stewart Clay Co., 133 Mulberry St., New York, New York

Jack D. Wolfe Co., Inc., 724 Meeker Ave., Brooklyn, New York

Ceramic Art Supply Co., 44 Groves St., New York, New York

DYES AND PIGMENTS

Fezandie & Sperrie, 103 Lafayette St., New York, New York

EPOXY RESINS

Schwartz Chemical Co., Inc., 50-01 Second St., Long Island City, New York

MARBLE & SLATE

Available from local monumental masons and builders' suppliers. Consult your local classified telephone directory.

TOOLS, GROUT, MASTIC, ADHESIVES:

Available at local artists' materials stores or from:
Beigert Co., 4801 Lemmon Ave., Dallas, Texas
Dillon Supply Co., 158 Eleventh St., San Francisco, California
Gager's Handicraft, 1024 Nicollet St., Minneapolis 3, Minnesota
Latco Products, 3371 Glendale Blvd., Los Angeles, California
Reynold Vedovato Corp., 725 E. 135th St., Bronx, New York

INDEX

Acetone, 19, 21
Adhesives, 13, 20-21; *see also* Epoxy resin; Glue; Mastic; Paste;
    Polyvinyl acetate glue
Aluminum, 24, 102
Applique, 137
Assemblage, 24, 83; illus. of, 12
Assemblage encaustic, illus. of, 2

Baking soda, 22, 23, 32, 34
Ball, F. Carlton, demo by, 96-102
Beeswax, 3
Black mastic, 19
Blackstrap molasses, *see* Molasses
Bowl, 24, 58
Brass, 24
Brown, Donna Jean, illus. by, 161
Brush, 22, 23, 30, 37
Builder's cloth, 24, 25, 58, 63, 75
Burg, Patricia, illus. by, 124
Burlap, 117
Buttering, 25, 31, 32, 37, 102
Byzantine enamel tesserae, 18
Byzantine tesserae, 33, 45, 58

Cardboard, 23, 62, 110
Cartoon, 29, 30, 32; *see also* Sketch
Casados, Victor, 20;
Casein glue, 21
Cement, 18, 20, 21, 42, 46, 58, 90, 98, 100, 130; epoxy, 19;
    gray, 22; latex, 19; plaster, 46; plastic, 49; Portland, 20, 22,
    46; stucco, 31; white, 19, 22, 46
Ceramic mosaic, 97-105
Ceramic tile, 18
Chalk, 110
Charcoal, 32
Cheesecloth, 20
Chisel, 58, 63; scoop, 23, 110
Clay, 102, 104; Barnard, 97
Cleaning, 34; mosaics, 22
Clement, Brooks, 129-130
Clippers, 46, 48

Collage, 46, 137; paper, 42
Composition board, 21
Concrete, 20
Copper, 24
Cutting tools, 19-20

Detergent, 22
Dike, Betty, illus. by, 88, 89
Dike, Phil, 88
Direct method, 26, 45-55; materials for, 19
Dow Chemical Company, 21
Drill, electric, 23
Drying, 22

Eggshell mosaics, 136
Elliot, Joe, illus. by, 56
Endomosaic, 95
Engobe, 104
Epoxy cement, 19
Epoxy resin, 3, 13, 20-21, 73, 104, 110, 125, 130

Finishing, 21-22; materials, 20-21
Firing, see Kiln
Flour, 30; rye, 32, 37, 42; wheat, 20
Found objects, 19, 77-95, 136
Frankel, Dextra, illus. by, 43, 69

Garrett, Allen, illus. by, 44
Garnet paper, 24, 110; see also Sandpaper
General Mills, Chemical Division of, 21
Gesso, 152
Glass, 18, 52, 73, 74, 130; colored, 18; cutting, 18, 19; flaws in, 19; painting, 18
Gloves, 32; rubber, 22
Glue, 20, 25, 30, 114; casein, 21; Wilhold, 86; see also Adhesives; Polyvinyl acetate glue
Goggles, 22, 23, 32
Greenberg, Janice, illus. by, 26, 84, 85
Grout, 20, 21, 22, 24, 31, 108
Grouting, 21-22, 34, 129
Gruenberg, Stephanie, illus. by, 140, 141
Gum arabic, 20, 31

Hammer, 58, 59, 63; hutch, 19, 31; scaling, 19, 31
Hardware cloth, see Builder's cloth
Hydrochloric acid, see Muriatic acid
Hydrocal, 24, 58, 75
Hutch hammer, 19, 31
Hutchinson, Mabel, 114; illus. by, 114, 115

Indirect method, 26, 29-44, 129; materials for, 19
Inlay, 129

Kefauver, Mrs. Estes, 90
Kiln, 98, 102, 104, 125
Knife, mat, 30; palette, 22, 23, 25, 37, 58, 102, 125, 126, 127; putty, 23, 46

Lane, Harriet, illus. by, 42
Latex cement, 20
Lemon, Chris, illus. by, 79, 80-81, 82
Library of Congress, 117
Library paste, 23
Lighting, 17
Lime, 20, 21-22, 46
Lovoos, Janice, illus. by, 53, 152, 153
Luitjens, Helen, 142, 148; illus. by, 68, 70, 139, 152

McKee, Dorothy, 138, 149, 155
McMillin, Tom, 104; illus. by, 105
Malcolm, Bonnie Jean, 102; demo by, 125-128; illus. by, 103
Manganese dioxide, 98, 102
Magnesite, 20, 42, 58, 63, 64, 125
Magnesium chloride, 20, 58
Mastic, 20, 25, 33-34, 37, 38, 102; black, 19, 125, 126
Marble dust, 24, 52
Marble tesserae, 18, 75
Marine plywood, 22, 102
Marme, see Marble tesserae
Masking tape, 25, 30
Masonite, 3, 13, 22, 42
Materials, 17-26 passim
Mat knife, 30
Metal, 21, 24
Michaels, Glen, illus. by, 54-55, 91, 92, 93, 106
Mitchell, Mr. and Mrs. Joseph, 45
Molasses, 37; blackstrap, 20, 30, 32, 42
Mortar, 20, 25
Museum of Contemporary Art, 117
Murals, 104; demonstrated, 29-32
Muriatic acid, 22, 23, 34

Nails, 24, 67, 71, 104, 117-123, 135
Nippers, cut, 19, 102
Norman, Emile, 129-130; illus. by, 73, 90, 95, 131, 132

Ortlieb, Robert, demo by, 110-113
Otis Art Institute, 57, 83
Oxide, black copper, 102; red iron, 98, 100, 102

Paints, 136
Palette knife, 22, 23, 25, 37, 58, 102, 125, 126, 127
Panel, preparing the, 30
Paper, 19, 110; garnett, 24, 110; mosaics, 137-138; press, 30; tracing, 23, 32, 42, 137
Partridge, David, 117-118; illus. by, 71, 116, 119, 120-121, 122-123
Paste, 23, 137
Paste wax, 23, 102
Pencil, 46, 60, 99, 137
Penny, Melissa, illus. of, 134
Permanex, 149
Plaster, 21, 125; cement, 46; of Paris, 24
Plastic, 19, 21, 130; cement, 49
Plexiglas, 95
Pliers, 19

Plywood, 22, 24, 25, 33, 44, 46, 49, 84, 98, 104, 110, 114, 117, 136; marine, 22, 102
Polishing, 34, 108
Polyester resin, 77, 83
Polyvinyl acetate glue, 21, 84, 88, 136
Putty knife, 23, 46

Rag, 22, 24, 34, 58, 138
Reducing glass, 24, 25
Reverse method, *see* Indirect method
Riffler, 23, 110
Rubber cement, 137

Salzer, Kayla, demo by, 46-59; illus. by, 60
Sand, 18, 21, 22, 46, 57-66 *passim*, 75
Sandcasting, 74, 75; method of, 57-66; illus. of, 16
Sander, electric, 23
Sandpaper, 23, 24, 110; *see also* Garnet paper
Scaling hammer, 19, 31
Schlein, Charles, 108; illus. by, 108-109, 133
Schools, mosaic techniques for, 135-161
Scissors, 137
Scoop chisel, 23
Screw driver, 23
Sculpture, mosaic, 125-133
Sealer, 24, 25, 33, 37
Secunda, Arthur, illus. by, 76, 83
Setting materials, 20-21
Seyle, Robert, demo by, 57-66; illus. by, 16, 67
Shell Chemical Company, 21
Shellac, 24, 25, 143
Shulman, Morris, illus. by, 12
Silver, 130
Sketch, 30, 34, 46, 47, 57-58, 88, 110, 118, 136; *see also* Cartoon
Smalti, *see* Byzantine enamel tesserae
Smith, John, Illus. by, 86, 87
Spackle, 21
Sponge, 22, 23, 24, 34, 38, 125
Spray, 68, 71

Stain, 24, 25, 58, 65, 114
Starrett Company, L.S., 19
Steel wool, 22, 24
Stewart, Jack, illus. by, 72, 75
Storage, 17, 18
Stucco, 20, *see* Cement; Mortar
Styrofoam, 24, 68, 71, 136
Supports, 22; *see also* Masonite; Plywood

Table, 17
Tate Gallery, 117
Tesserae, applying, 32-33; cutting, 19-20; defined, 18; pasting, 30-31; *see also* Byzantine tesserae; Ceramic tile; Glass; Marble; Venetian glass
Texture, 17, 46-47, 118
Tin, 24
Tin snips, 46
Tools, 17-26 *passim*
Toothbrush, 110
Torch, 3
Trowel, 23, 31, 33, 46, 49, 104
Turpentine, 19, 22, 23, 24, 58, 65
Tweezers, 22, 23, 112

University of Southern California, 97

Varnish, 24, 86
Venetian Art Mosaics, Inc., 29; illus. of studio, 28
Venetian glass tesserae, 18, 33, 45, 58
Versimid, 21

Wax, 73; paste, 23, 102
White glue, 68; *see* Polyvinyl acetate glue
Wilhold glue, 86
Wood, 21, 23, 107-115 *passim*, 130, 133, 135; mosaics, 107-115
Woolett, Janice, illus. by, 74
Work area, 17-18
Work bench, 17

Edited by Donald Holden
Technical editing by Jack Stewart
Designed by Museum Planning, Inc.

Photocomposition in Ten Point Melior by Noera-Rayns Studio, Inc.

Printed and bound in Japan by Toppan Printing Co., Ltd.